Thriving In CHAOS

Thriving In
CHAOS

Reclaim the joy in your crazy life!

Tracy A. Knofla

First Printing: November 2007

Library of Congress Control Number 2007940964

ISBN 978-0-615-17453-2

Printed and Manufactured in the United States of America
High Impact Training, St. Cloud, Minnesota 56302

To learn more about High Impact Training or to order additional copies
of Thriving in Chaos email us at info@hit4you.net or call 320-259-8222.

Cover Design: Peg Churchwell, Lady Dog Design, Long Prairie, MN

Cover Photo: Jim Altobell, Altobell Imagery, Waite Park, MN

Cover Model: Amanda Henry, Cold Spring, MN

Inside Design: Karen Ritter, Continental Press, St. Cloud, MN

Dedication

This book is dedicated to my dear friend, Bobbie Wittmer. Bobbie, you are a consummate professional and have been a mentor to me in more ways than you know. You believed in my talent before I ever did and have been an indefatigable supporter. I love you Bobbie and thank you for the blessing of your friendship.

Table of Contents

– With Gratitude –

The production of this book has been a joy and a pain in equal measure. It has been a group effort in many ways. There are plenty of people to thank for helping me to stay focused, sound literate, and keep my sense of humor.

Primary on this list has been the team at High Impact Training. My business partner and friend of over twenty years, Mark Geller, as well as Sarah Ostvig, Melanie Hartman, Amanda Schneider, Amanda Henry and Sara Lichliter. You all have been invaluable to me, especially in these final months of writing. You make me proud to be associated with you!

In addition to our primary staff, we have enjoyed much success due to the efforts of four very special people. Diane Hageman and Peg Churchwell are to be thanked for helping our company develop its unique look and perspective. Julie Merkle has made sure we stay fiscally strong and sensible. And Jeff Nemens always asks the tough questions that make Mark and I go "Huh?" but that ultimately lead us to where we need to go. You have all played a huge role in our company's success.

This book is not just my dream. It is a dream shared by us all!

Over the course of my professional career there have been so many people who have taught or influenced me. You are, for better or worse, responsible for who I am today. Too numerous to name here, I just say a grateful "thank you." However, there are two people who, over 15 years ago, started speaking "Thriving in Chaos" language with me and helped me to fully realize the concept of thriving. dr. beth triplett and Meri Phillips, I thank you both so very much!

I must thank the thousands of people who have taught me about the nature of chaos and its impact on their lives—the wonderful audiences of my "Thriving in Chaos" workshops. Your input has formed many of the tips in this book. I have enjoyed laughing with and learning from you!

Two very creative and brilliant people gave me a renewed interest in finishing this book and were instrumental in making sure the grammar in the book is correct. Roland and Lynn Chirico read the initial drafts and were kind and supportive of this author's fragile ego. You two gave me the energy boost I needed to finish and a great laugh as I watched you argue over points of grammar!

Special thanks go to my family and to my friends who have become as close to me as family. I will write all of your names here if I need to fill more pages! But basically if I have: cooked you a meal, hosted you on the deck, laughed with you, played with your kids, or served you a blender drink—you know I'm talking abut you! Thanks for providing me with your real-life examples to teach others about chaos. We've shared great laughs, dances, recipes, swims in the lake, walks with the dogs, volleyball in the "hood," and in the case of Carolyn and Bettina, a nearly life-long history. All of these things are the greatest gifts I have ever received and I love you all—but you still have to buy the book!

Finally, I truly believe everyone needs someone who can give them wings and keep them tethered, when each is required. For me, Karen, you are the one! Thank you for putting up with my nomadic ways, for walking the dog at 10 p.m. in the rain when I am on the road, and for always being happy when I return. I couldn't do any of this without you!

Thriving in Chaos—
Is This Even Possible?

Just mention the title of this book to your friends and watch their reactions. You will hear everything from, "That's the story of my life," to "My boss needs to read that book!" It seems everyone, in this day and age, has some chaos they must endure.

> *The American Heritage Dictionary* defines chaos as:
> *1. A condition or place of great disorder or confusion.*
> *2. A disorderly mass; a jumble.*

I'm sure many of you define chaos as: *1. waking up at 5 a.m. to get your children out of the house by 7 a.m.; 2. feeding the family and the animals; 3. working long hours; 4. managing a household; 5. caring for grandchildren or elderly parents; 6. not getting enough sleep; 7. eating the wrong foods and; 8. always feeling like you have to catch up.*

This book will help you—if you let it! Look at the difference between the definition of the word chaos and this definition of the word thrive.

To thrive is:

1. To make steady progress; prosper.

2. To grow vigorously; flourish.

Do you feel that these two concepts are incompatible? I don't, and it's my job from this point on to help you see that it IS possible for you to "grow vigorously and flourish" even during a "condition of great disorder or confusion."

In the following pages you will come to understand the nature of the chaos that surrounds you. You will see that there are consequences to chaos run amok. You will learn skills to help you make the most out of every circumstance. You will even be challenged to create a plan of action.

I thank you for reading this book. By doing so, you are planting the seeds that will help you to "grow vigorously" and ultimately, "flourish." Enjoy! After you do, please share it with your friends.

"Asking me why I need a book about 'Thriving in Chaos' is like asking why a plant needs water. I want to thrive!"

Meleia Jordan, Flight Attendant, Northwest Airlines

Why all of this Chaos?

There are many factors responsible for the chaos we are experiencing today. Some may be out of your control, but let's see if any of these apply to you.

* The Pace of the World

* Our Abundant/Overwhelming Choices

* A Complex Family/Home Life

* Even More Complex Work Life

* E-Mail and Personal Technology Explosion

* Our Acquisition Mentality

* Unease With Leisure and Free Time

* Information Overload

The Pace of the World

As this book is written, the new millennium is hitting its stride. It's a grand time, to be sure, but one in which the pace of everything has exceeded our ability to keep up. Technology has created an "instant expectation" within society. We can't wait for a "dial-up connection" for our computer—we need high-speed Internet. We want to purchase goods that will arrive overnight, even if we purchase them online at midnight. We expect instant service from providers, and if they can't comply—we simply move on to someone who can. All of these set up a "do it/get it, now" expectation in our world. It is too fast for most of us.

> *"There is no 'down time' anymore at the office or home. We used to be able to count on certain months out of the year as being slower than others. This is no longer true."*
>
> Mary Geller, Vice President for Student Development, College of St. Benedict, MN

Our Abundant/Overwhelming Choices

Run, don't walk to the nearest grocery store. The store is the size of a football field, so be sure to wear your running shoes. Once there, slow down and take some time to let the overwhelming number of choices sink in. In the produce section alone, you can choose vegetables that are organic or non-organic, native or imported, and varieties of the same item. Move on to the soup aisle where instead of one or two brands, there are hundreds of options.

All over the grocery store, you will find the most basic "staples" in a huge variety of price, calories, fat content, etc. My favorite example—however, not my favorite experience—is to go to the pharmacy aisle for a cold remedy. *(Please go there with a cold to experience the full effect.)* Standing amidst the seemingly endless aisle of cold relief products, I feel worse than when I entered and woefully under-educated as to the difference between decongestants and expectorants! *"I have a cold. I just want something to fix it, please!"*

"Life is chaotic because there are so many choices—many of them good choices and so it gets harder and harder to prioritize."

dr. beth triplett,
Vice President for Enrollment,
Maryville University, St. Louis

These examples of consumerism help us see that while we are grateful for the abundance these choices allow us it takes significantly more time to process all of these variables and (eventually) make a decision. No wonder so many people hate to go shopping!

Food, a favorite and recurring theme in this book, is just one of many examples of our abundant choices. Furniture, clothing, home decorations, digital gadgets, movies to rent, television channels, and magazines are a few of the other things that demonstrate this abundance.

A Complex Family/Home Life

According to the Bureau of Labor Statistics, over half of married American couples have both father and mother in the workforce. An average of 80 percent of single parents work as well.[1] Wow!

Keeping the home running smoothly used to be a full time job. Cleaning house, making dinner, chauffeuring children to one or two activities weekly used to fill the entire workday. The full time job of running the household has not lessened. In many cases it has increased. What has lessened is the time in which it can now be accomplished.

"Cleaning my house de-clutters my brain!"

Diane Heriot, Jewelry Designer/Waitress

How do your household chores get done? Choose all that apply to you:

1. **with a supportive partner**

2. **by you in the wee hours of the morning**

3. **with the help of fast food takeout (curbside)**

4. **by engaging the services of a housekeeper**

5. **using an overburdened family calendaring system**

6. **they don't get done!**

No matter the method, the home life is still very complicated. It needs much attention, and the hours between the end of one workday and bedtime are too few to handle it all.

Let's not even start talking about the children's activities, which have exploded in recent years: lessons, tutoring, sports, band, and specialized before and after school programs, etc. Keeping track of all of these activities requires its own database!

In fact, I got a glimpse of just how complicated today's home life is during a conversation with my neighbor, Wendy. She was thrilled that she had finally secured the necessary day care arrangements for the youngest of her three children. She excitedly explained that on Monday her daughter Lily would be here. On Tuesday, she would be there, and on Wednesday she would be yet another place. And then, of course, I learned that her husband John picks up James and Tessa another day and drops them off to the neighbor's for a play date. Even with her positive attitude, I realized that today's family faces incredibly complex time and life management issues.

> *"Ah, the schedule of life—family activities, kids' homework and practice schedules, work obligations, friendships, personal health, volunteer work, and, oh, yes, even my husband need a little time and attention! I try to embrace chaos rather than allowing it to control me!"*
>
> Tamie Klumpyan, Klumpyan Family Muli-tasker and
> Editor/Event Coordinator, PaperClip Communications

Even More Complex Work Life

The reality of today's workplace is this—more work, fewer people to do it! Downsizing of staff, severe budget cuts, and enhanced technology all help account for the chaos you may feel in the workplace. Not only that, but the pressure to be faster and more cutting edge than your competitors, as well as your own desire to be perfect within the workplace, may contribute to your feelings of being overwhelmed.

"Chaos is part of everyone's life. The challenge is to determine who is in charge, you or the chaos that has become part of you."

John Green, President, COO, Coldwell Banker Griffith & Blair American Home, KS

Have you noticed, too, that the workplace has crept into your home life? Many of you can access your e-mail at home and regularly work for a couple of hours on projects you just can't finish at work. Are you on duty 24/7?

E-mail and Personal Technology Explosion

E-mail gets its own paragraph here as a "chaos causer." Many of you regularly express your feelings of being overwhelmed by the barrage of e-mail you receive daily. The sheer number and implied immediacy of this messaging system, makes you hesitate before taking a vacation or even taking a needed sick day. You say, *"I just can't face all of the e-mails when I return."* So you don't leave, or you read them at home from your sickbed. I'll offer some hints about how to manage e-mail in the Thriving Tips section of this book.

It's not just e-mail, however. There has also been an explosion in the number of electronic and digital gadgets that help you be more efficient. There are devices to help you to enjoy your own music or that allow you to download television shows and podcasts. There are "personal digital assistants" with fruity names that allow you to read your e-mail and surf the Internet while you are on the go. These electronic playthings are fun, but they all have batteries and need to be "docked" somewhere or "synched" to something. And of course that's after you learn how to use them all!

Our Acquisition Mentality

Because there are now so many choices of things to buy, many of you do! Is it bad? Not necessarily; however, it does contribute to your chaos (even though some of you will swear that it is a stress reducer!) Acquiring things for the sake of having them—to make your life happier or your home prettier—brings with it its own unique concerns.

First, how are you paying for that new dining room set? Financing, low-interest credit cards, second or third mortgages? How soon before the mounting debt from all that you acquire causes you chaos? We need only tune into one of the many home improvement channels to see that once we acquire this stuff, we are at a loss as to how to store it.

The self-store-it industry reports that nearly one in ten U.S. households currently rents a self-storage unit. This represents an increase of approximately 65 percent in the last 12 years.[2] Looks like we have way more stuff to store, organize, dust, and maintain. Plus, more debt to show for it all. UGH!

Is it bad to surround yourself with beautiful or cool things? Not necessarily, but as William Morriss, 19th century architect, stated so well,

> *"Have nothing in your house that you do not know to be useful or believe to be beautiful."* [3]

Make that your mantra!

Unease with Leisure and Free Time

When I attended college in the late '70's, my professors and textbooks in the Recreation and Leisure department taught me that we would become a "leisure society" within 20 years. They claimed the need for trained leisure counselors would be great because people would work less and have more free time. Things sure have changed from those predictions! Now we need leisure counselors to help people to "unplug" and value their non-work time.

We are a society that acknowledges the need to recharge our cell phone, pager, Blackberry, iPod, and computer batteries, but not our own inner batteries! All work and no play makes not just Jack, but everyone dull. More than that, such an unbalance is potentially dangerous to our physical health and spiritual well being. German playwright, Johann Wolfgang Von Goethe, nailed it when he said,

"We must always change, renew, rejuvenate ourselves; otherwise we harden." [4]

Rejuvenation, whether by a two-week vacation or daily meditation, is necessary to the human spirit, both in the long run and on a daily basis. The "Energizer Bunny" does need occasional recharging—even if you never see it in the commercials!

Information Overload

Twenty-four hour TV news. Access to over 42 million web servers, your choice of 1400 newspapers, or a circulation of 10,000 magazines.[5] This doesn't even count the explosion of blogs and podcasts produced annually. Just reading the research compiled by Sarah Ostvig in our office has given me information overload!

We are the best-informed society ever, yet we often feel burdened rather than empowered by this information. We have so much information available to us, but no time to adequately process it to give our lives meaning.

"I am not convinced that all the advances in technology serve to advance or simplify my life. In fact, on occasion I think just the opposite—the gateway of information has led to endless hours of unproductive inquiry. It is time we all learn more about how to navigate this unending stream of information."

Ken Brill, Associate Dean of Students, Augustana College

Consequences
of this Chaos

Have you cried UNCLE? Do you want to light an aromatherapy candle and hide under your duvet and matching sheet set until the world changes again? Hopefully not, but perhaps some of these causal factors resonate with you and make you want to delve deeper.

Say it! Say your life is chaotic!

Easy words–in fact many people say them daily–but without conviction or any intention of changing things. Let's look at the consequences of this chaos in an effort to further convince you of the need to make a change.

"It doesn't have to be this crazy – no matter how organized I try to be, my life seems to get more complicated each day."

Bettina Ferguson, Director of Finance & Assistant Treasurer, CRRA, CT

Physical Symptoms

Have you left work early with a headache or developed one when you walked in the door at home? The Tylenol  Company estimates that 45 million Americans suffer from recurrent headaches each year. Tension headaches account for 90 percent of them.[6]

The therapeutic massage industry reports that 25 million more Americans get a massage today then they did ten years ago.[7] According to the 2002 National Health Interview Survey, nearly 20 percent of the U. S. population has used chiropractic care at some point, and 7.5 percent of the adult population in the U.S. has chiropractic care each year.[8]

My favorite of all—the day spa industry—has exploded. The International Spa Association reports that there were nearly eleven thousand day spas in the U.S. in 2005, up 16 percent over the previous two years. Revenue figures show that the industry receives approximately $6.7 billion annually. In 2006 there were 110 million visits to some type of spa.[9] It seems we all are feeling the effects of stress and chaos.

Fatigue and feelings of sadness accounted for nearly 32 billion dollars in lost wages and productivity, according to a 2002 study.[10] Continuous stress can contribute to overeating, decreased physical activity, smoking and excessive drinking—tall of which can have major physical consequences to our health and well-being.

Psychological/Emotional Consequences

Our self-esteem suffers when we live in perpetual chaos. Feelings of inadequacy can result from an unending and unfinished to-do list. There is often little joy and celebration for our accomplishments (or even modest recognition of them) because we move so hurriedly on to the next task.

The overwhelming number of choices available may cause us to become paralyzed and inactive. The sheer volume of work, both in our job and within our home life, can make us feel that nothing is interesting, exciting or rewarding. Boredom, disengagement, and the inability to manage our basic emotions are inevitable. We lose the joy in life.

Professional Consequences

Your career may suffer as the chaos continues. When tapped for a promotion or asked to accept more responsibility, you may feel less willing to accept it, less able to manage it, and may experience reduced performance because of it.

You may lose your focus or become inattentive to the details. Unless you are highly organized, you may forget projects or deadlines. Your attitude and work may suffer, as might your future earning potential.

On Your Children

Are we placing the same demanding standards that we expect of ourselves on our children? Some children report feeling stressed out as early as the 3rd or 4th grade. Pre-teenage children are being given day planners as gifts to help them manage their multiple priorities.

> *"As a junior at a prep school, I get home late and have hours of homework to do—needless to say I am stressed!"*
>
> Elizabeth Hackett, High School Student, Loomis Chaffee School

Has chaos affected the quality or quantity of time spent with your children? And has this feeling of constantly being overwhelmed impacted your discipline system with them? Many parents report that they "just can't deal with disciplining their children at the end of a long day." Are there consequences to this? You bet!

Your Intimate Personal Relationships

What role might this chaos play in your ability to establish and maintain an intimate personal relationship? Are you too tired from a hectic day at work to go to the places where there might be other singles? Does the overwhelming amount of work that faces you at home each night—after that long day at work outside of the home—leave you feeling exhausted, frustrated, angry or resentful? Does lack of time for yourself leave you feeling unattractive, thus dampening your desire to be intimate with your partner? Do you find it difficult to create time for you and your partner to converse about non-child or work-related issues?

The American divorce rate is currently at 38 percent, although the U.S. Census Bureau has cited it as high as 50 percent.[11] If you watch daytime television (i.e., Jerry Springer, Divorce Court, or the "soaps"), you might see that many people who are in a primary relationship are not happy with their partner. I think the chaos of the world has made it more difficult to find that special someone. And once you do, the chaos hovers around, threatening the stability of your relationship.

Our Friendships and Social Relationships

Humans are social creatures; yet, are you finding it increasingly difficult to schedule time with close friends? Have you experienced a loss of intimacy with your friends and have you tried to replace this intimacy with other people (with varying degrees of success)?

Friendships are vital to a healthy individual. Yet, have you found spending time with your friends has become a to-do-list chore instead of a source of rejuvenation?

This loss of intimacy with trusted friends can also result in inappropriate workplace relationships (romances) and over-sharing of details with relative strangers. It is estimated that 28 million Americans have visited Internet chat rooms to discuss everything from weight loss to cocker spaniels.[12] I wonder if this virtual contact is ultimately as satisfying to us as human contact with those we care about.

On Our Community at Large

Too busy to volunteer for the PTA, the scouting programs, to coach your child's soccer team? Too exhausted to think

of running for public office or to attend a public forum about civic affairs? Local governments are experiencing a lack of volunteers to serve on important boards. Lewis Feldstein, co-author of the article "Better Together: Restoring the American Community," says people's willingness to volunteer in their communities decreases by 10 percent for each additional 10 minutes they drive to work."[13]

This lack of time or energy for civic affairs impacts our foundation of beliefs as citizens. When you are too busy to volunteer in your community, you allow a smaller group of people to speak for you and deny your children the opportunity to see you as a strong community advocate.

Do you read a local paper to keep up with community news? Circulation for local papers is down nationally. The annual report on American journalism from journalism.org states that the number of local newspapers remained constant from the 1940's until the early 1980's. Since the 80's, however, there has been a 17 percent decrease in the number of local newspapers and an 11 percent drop in circulation within just the last 12 years.[14] Given this, the potential for disconnect with your local community is great.

On the Economy

Is there an economic impact caused by all of this chaos? I think so. Look all around you for these clues:

> * absenteeism
>
> * sleep-deprivation related accidents
>
> * workplace violence
>
> * workplace affairs
>
> * management staff that are unable to handle employee issues
>
> * employees who do not bring new ideas to the workplace for fear of "having to do all of the work"

The workplace isn't the only place we see the economic impact. A decrease in the number of personal savings and retirement funds and an increase in debt and personal bankruptcy may be caused by unresolved chaos. I "Googled" the topic of "personal debt" and found over three million entries. Is this a chicken-and-egg situation? Is the chaos caused by a slow economy forcing us to work harder, or do we contribute to the economic chaos by not taking control of our fiscal lives?

Are You
Addicted to Chaos?

We all know someone who seems to need a high degree of "drama" or chaos in his life to help him appear important. Many years ago I had a work colleague who, while a wonderful person, always attended our professional meetings late and with an outrageous story about some crisis that had just occurred in his workplace. At first we were sympathetic, listening to the issue and engaging in time-consuming brainstorming and counseling sessions to help solve the problem. He seemed to thrive during these meetings. But, then, a slow reckoning occurred.

At the fourth meeting he attended, late and with stories, we realized that something was really wrong. Not that we doubted the truth of what he was saying. We believed him to be truthful. But we realized this pattern of behavior was not normal. All of us worked in the same profession, faced the same kinds of issues, but none of us had the same reaction to it. It was then that we realized our colleague was addicted to chaos. He literally needed to have these crises in order to make him feel necessary, needed or important.

Who is this person in your life? Hope it's not you. Is chaos a part of life in the new millennium? Yes! Do we need a little chaos to keep us on our toes? Yes! Can chaos help you to be more productive or more professional or teach you new things? Absolutely! I see value in chaos. However, I also see chaos as a crutch some people lean on in order to avoid facing certain personal truths or to avoid taking action.

Talking about the chaos gives you something to complain about, and we are experts in listening to others' complaints. Go to lunch tomorrow with your work colleague or your close friend and see how long it takes before he starts to complain about his job, boss, kids, spouse, house, salary, weeds, in-laws, etc. Of course with trusted friends and colleagues you know it's important to be able to vent. We all vent, and we need to from time to time. The casual complainers are not those to whom I refer.

Look around your lunch group. Who is the one who always starts it? Who is the one who is always bending your ear? This is the person most likely addicted to chaos. As with any addiction, chaos addicts must want to change their behavior. And until they ask for help in doing so, this book will sit on the bookshelf collecting dust.

As you identify those around you who might be "addicted to chaos", I ask you to think about your reaction to their displays. Do you find yourself getting upset about your life when you hear them go on and on? Do you get emotionally involved in their situations and think about them long after your lunch is over? Or do you take the interaction for what it is—an opportunity for a friend to vent or gain needed attention and then shake it off after it is over? Hopefully you do not let the habitual problems of your friends or coworkers interfere with your outlook on life and your motivation to thrive.

> "Without a certain amount of uncontrolled chaos in our lives, we would not be able to thrive and grow with the controlled chaos that we call everyday life!"
>
> Christiaan Didden,
> Government Relations
> Consultant

If you have persons in your life who drain your energy with their addiction to chaos, try setting some parameters with them. When they begin complaining, you might say, "I'm glad to talk about these issues with you for half of our lunch break, then let's talk about our vacations or our children's accomplishments, or some other shared positive experience." It might sound awkward at first, and you might need to try several approaches before it works; but you will see changes if you are consistent.

For those reading this book who see their own addiction to chaos, I ask you to try to honestly identify what it is you get from the chaos and find healthy and positive ways to achieve the same goals. There will be many helpful suggestions as you continue reading this book.

Choose to Thrive

The potential consequences of this chaos, as I hope you have seen, are many and far-reaching. It is not my intention to be an alarmist. But let's face it; you did see yourself in some of the areas mentioned. You have already felt the weight of some of these consequences. It is now time to move on and see that there are many, many ways to thrive!

This book was written specifically for those who want to change their life in some big or small way. It was written for those who want to be even more happy, fulfilled and successful in their chaos. I hope that person is YOU! Ultimately, it is your choice.

It's Your Choice

You might find it curious that I include a chapter on making choices when I cite the overwhelming number of choices in our world as a chaos-causing factor. But the fact is, when you make a conscious choice about something you feel better. Simple as that! You buy into the choice and support the feelings or actions necessary to complete the choice.

Some choices are easy. Plain, Peanut or Crispy M&Ms. When you are offered these choices at a party for instance, you eat the chosen type with a bit more gusto than if you had just been offered one type. Many of you are settling for what others offer you, instead of making intentional choices.

When you are invited on a date to the movies and get to pick the show, you become a bit more invested in how the experience turns out. If someone asks you on that same date for a movie they have selected, you may not be as invested.

> "I look at all the chaos I juggle on a daily basis, working 30 hours a week, attending college full time, having a boyfriend, friends, family, cleaning up after 3 messy roommates and a dog. Some days I just want to give up! Most days, I just want more choices!"
>
> Amanda Schneider, College Student, Account Executive, High Impact Training

The principle of choice holds true for many areas of your life.

> * If you choose to go on a diet, you might stick with it longer than if your doctor tells you to diet.
>
> * If your child picks out his own clothes, he will dress himself more readily.
>
> * College students study harder for a major of their own choice, rather than one of their parents.
>
> * Work projects of your choice are accomplished more quickly than those that are arbitrarily assigned to you.

Along with the power of this choice comes responsibility and consequences.

> * If the movie you chose was a dud—you chose it.
>
> * If your diet was unrealistic and failed—you chose it.
>
> * If the work project became much more time consuming than you expected—you chose it.

On the other hand:

> * **If the movie is great—you chose it.**
>
> * **If the diet is successful—you chose it.**
>
> * **When the work project is a hit—you chose it.**

Look at the power you have—either way!

Why We Won't Choose

Fear of the consequences of the choices you make may cause you not to choose at all. Fear of being wrong, wasting time, not having support, or failing, all enter into the decision making process—consciously or subconsciously. It is easier to blame our circumstances and play the role of the "victim" than to own our responsibility for a bad choice.

For instance, the outline for this book (and three others) had been around for longer than two years before I started actually writing it. The fear of failure, fear of success, personal laziness, coupled with a grueling travel schedule, were all excuses I used not to write this book.

Yet, it is very important that this book exists—for both you and me! My conscious choice and subsequent actions finally made it happen! And I feel great because of it! It might have been easier to continue making excuses for not writing this book; but, ultimately, I feel better because I did finish it than I ever did *not writing it.*

Before You Choose

So what do you want? You need to answer this question before you can make a choice about anything. My good friend and fellow training consultant, Michael Miller, asks people this question in a workshop of the same name, *"What do you want from your time and your life?"* He is persistent and masterful at helping people identify what they truly want. Their first, second and third answers often do not accurately identify what they really want. Michael makes them dig deeper to find the right answer for themselves.

Before even asking this question, however, you need to believe that you are worthy of answering it, that you deserve to make choices for a better life. Easy or not, you deserve the chance to try to thrive in your world, as opposed to settling for what other people want or for what the world offers you. Believe in your right to have choices and then feel the power that comes with it.

Easy or Not

Many choices can be categorized as easy or not. Think of the small daily choices you make—what to wear, what to have for breakfast, what kind of coffee to order, where to walk the dog, how early or late to

arrive at work, etc. Although what is an easy choice in one situation may not be in another. If you have a big presentation at work, what you wear might not be an easy choice, just as what to have for breakfast can be a difficult choice if you are frustrated by your weight.

More often than not, the easier choices are those that involve just you. Add family or co-workers into the mix, and the choices may become more difficult.

The more complex choices, whether to go for the promotion, or to confront a non-supportive partner, or to move your family to a new state, are tougher. But once made, again, regardless of the outcome, give you tremendous power. All the more reason to embrace all of your choices!

This book will offer you countless choices for thriving in your chaos. Some will require large changes, others small ones. They will ultimately help you to feel more in control of your life. But honestly, it's up to you to choose the one or ones that sound most feasible. And then it will be up to you to follow through. Again,

it's your choice!

How do you choose the actions that will make the most sense for you? Here is a plan to help you sort through the myriad choices available.

1. **Clearly identify the problem or opportunity.**
2. **Take time to reflect on the situation and look at your options.**
3. **Set aside time to choose.**
4. **Find a trusted person with whom to share the idea with.**
5. **Pick one or two preliminary choices and create a plan of action—clearly anticipating likely outcomes.**
6. **Settle on the right choice and become empowered by it.**
7. **Evaluate your choice continually and adjust the plan accordingly.**

See the Choice—Feel the Power

When we feel victimized by all that happens around us, we surrender our power to others or abandon it altogether. The better way to regain control is to see the power that lies in our choices. We can choose our attitudes, our actions and our reactions more often than we realize. This choice is what separates the winners from the whiners.

For instance, I love to travel, and am still amazed that I can wake up in Connecticut and go to sleep in California in the same day. I travel by airplane to over 75 percent of the workshops I facilitate. This means that I am at the mercy of the airlines and dependent on them to get me where I need to be.

Believe me, I'd much rather drive to work. Behind the wheel, I am in control. Yet, I spend much of my time in major and not so major airports around the country and usually have lots of time to observe other passengers and airline personnel.

I particularly enjoy watching the process when there are weather delays. A weather delay is something no one can control. Yet, some passengers become enraged when they see a delay and take this out on the person behind the counter. I see lots of red faces and hear lots of demeaning comments. I imagine the blood pressures of both passengers and employees rising dramatically.

Do I enjoy being delayed? NO! But in that situation where, literally, it is out of any mere mortal's hands, I choose to keep my power and focus on my choice. I have chosen to work in a profession that involves handing

"Much of our life is not controllable... by learning we can choose our response to situations we can not only survive, but thrive, amidst the chaos."
Brenda Rohlfing, Human Resources Manager, MRCI Worksource

over control. Most of the time I am grateful to have this choice. However, when I feel chaos ready to take hold I realize that the choices I have are to...

---

1. **become emotional, either angry or frustrated for the next several hours and complain to everyone around me.**

2. **solve the problem, i.e., call the airlines, reschedule my flight, and call my host to inform them of the delay.**

3. **take out a good book and enjoy my new found leisure.**

I usually do number two, and then number three.

Which one do you choose in this situation?

How Do We Identify Our Choices?

The old adage, "You can't see the forest for the trees" is based in truth. If you've ever taken a walk in the forest, you will see that there is an entire ecosystem living under the canopy of leaves that define a forest. There are moss and lichen, ferns and tiny flowering plants, insects, squirrels, the occasional deer, and, more frequently, the droppings of unseen animals that confirm their existence in a seemingly deserted place. It would be a mistake to define the forest as simply a place with a lot of trees. Life flourishes in the forest.

As with the forest, it would be a mistake to define your life with simple descriptors that might suffice as happy-hour chitchat but do no justice to the complexity that is your life. You are not merely an employee, a partner, a wife or husband, a parent or sibling. Your life is not merely work, eat, sleep, work eat, sleep, and workeatsleep!

Within this life, you should not expect simplicity with either the problem or the solution. In fact, as noted creative wizard, Roger Von Oech, teaches in his famous book on creativity, *A Whack on the Side of the Head*, there is always more than one right answer to almost any question. And so, as you wonder about what causes the chaos in your life, I ask you to look for the second and third right answer that might be the real right answer for you.

For instance, you might say that your life is chaotic because both you and your husband work full time and are raising two kids. Okay, that's one answer. But another right answer might be that you want the house to look a certain way, and you insist on cleaning it yourself without the help of your spouse and kids. The third right answer might be that you are a workaholic who doesn't know how to relax and thus creates chaos where none really exists. Once you are honest with yourself about the real cause of your chaos, you begin to see the choices that will help you thrive.

At any given time you have lots of choices. For instance you can:

* ask for help
* drop one or more projects
* develop an organizational system to manage things more effectively
* hire out some services
* give up!

No matter which one you pick *(except, I hope, "give up"),* the simple process of identifying your options will make you feel stronger than before and open the door for more than one right answer to emerge.

Are You A SUPERSTAR?

I help people to see the effects of their chaos and the options available to them through a simple, yet effective demonstration. A volunteer I call the SUPERSTAR is asked to come on stage and hold some items until I tell her to put them down. The volunteer is usually very eager to complete the assignment and will comply with the request even before knowing the full extent of her responsibility. Other audience members are then invited on stage to give the SUPERSTAR some more items to hold—big, small, heavy and light. There are usually about 50 items weighing approximately 40-50 pounds total.

Typically, the SUPERSTAR won't question the assignment and will accept the items as delivered to her very cheerfully. *Enjoy the photos of previous superstars.*

She is then required to hold the items for approximately 10-15 minutes while the audience watches.

It's always fun to see how the SUPERSTAR reacts to this time consideration. And more fun to see how the audience reacts. Many lessons are learned from this demonstration, yet the most important one to emerge is the idea of choice.

The SUPERSTAR could choose to put everything down, could ask for help, or could just sit down. She could ask

> *"It's the sign of the times, we are juggling more than our parents and grandparents did—I'm a single mom, full-time higher ed. administrator, graduate student, church volunteer, sibling, and cat owner."*
> Tricia Nolfi, Associate Director University Human Resources, Rutgers University, NJ

for a big bag, (in fact, the bag that all of the materials arrived in is in plain sight under a nearby table.) But the SUPERSTAR more often than not just stands there, holding all of the items, until given permission by me to put them down or receives help from audience members who can't stand to see her suffer any more.

As we process the activity, all participants realize the impact of this burden on the SUPERSTAR and also the burdens they personally carry that may weigh them down. The SUPERSTAR often states that she did not realize she had options. She was just doing what she was asked to do and:

1. didn't want to disappoint me

2. didn't want to make waves

3. didn't want to appear incompetent in front of her peers

4. didn't want to lose a prize—even though she did not know what the prize was!

5. didn't want to let herself down

6. didn't want to be seen as irresponsible

7. didn't think she could do anything differently

8. didn't think she could ask for help or could modify the situation

9. didn't see any other way of being successful

10. didn't enjoy the experience any longer

This seemingly simple activity dramatically demonstrates the need for us to see our choices and is applicable to the chaos we feel in our everyday lives.

Have you ever FELT like our SUPERSTAR LOOKS? If so, it is time to teach you to THRIVE!

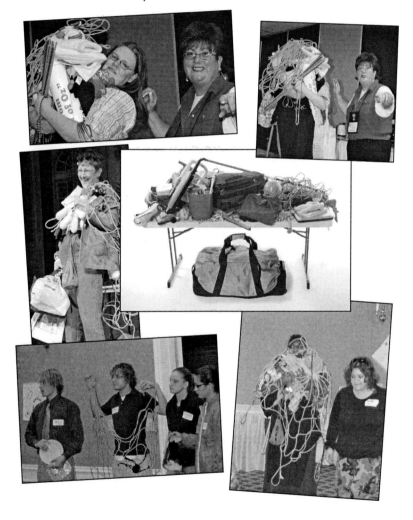

So Teach Me to Thrive Already!

In addition to identifying the choices available to you, I have identified 12 key concepts, which I believe will be invaluable as you start the process of thriving.

1. **Ask More Questions**
2. **Ask for Help**
3. **Offer Help to Others**
4. **Develop Systems to Help You Manage the Chaos**
5. **Take Time for Reflection**
6. **Set Limits on your Time and Activities**
7. **Keep Your Eye on the Prize**
8. **Seek Balance in Your Life**
9. **Thrive. Don't Just Cope**
10. **Look for "Everyday" Humor**
11. **Simplify, Simplify, Simplify**
12. **Take Life-Enhancing Risks**

Ask More Questions!

Ask more questions and seek more information before beginning any new task.

My SUPERSTAR, in her zeal to (a) be a volunteer (b) please me, (c) be the center of attention, (d) receive the fabulous prize, usually neglects to ask me anything of importance before taking on the responsibility. My directions are intentionally vague, "Please hold some objects without dropping them until I tell you to put them down." If she had asked me some questions prior to accepting this position, she might have felt differently about volunteering and certainly might have taken some control of the situation.

How often have you accepted a new task without asking many questions, only to regret it later? Why don't we ask more questions?

Many people won't ask questions for fear of the answer. For instance, if in your last job your supervisor was not open to answering questions and made you feel silly when you asked, you might be hesitant to ask your new supervisor any questions. You might risk doing something wrong rather than ask a question, fearing the reaction of your new supervisor.

> **THRIVING TIP:**
> Pay attention to the employee who is the most successful in getting his or her needs met. Identify their techniques and try them out yourself.

Where else does this fear come from? Maybe it's the fear of looking incompetent to your co-workers. Maybe it's the fear of a negative reaction from your family members. Maybe you want to be seen as the shining star who can handle everything—no matter the personal cost. Maybe we don't ask the question because it doesn't occur to us to ask. After all, years of accepting responsibilities without question have created powerful habits. These long held habits no longer serve most people.

The unasked question cannot help you thrive!

When you don't ask the necessary questions at work, you miss an opportunity for your supervisor to see that you value your time and the successful accomplishment of all projects under your care. You deny your supervisor an opportunity to be a "good guy" and, instead, paint him into the role of adversary. You deny yourself an opportunity to feel the satisfaction of sticking up for yourself and gaining some self-respect. You miss an opportunity to have honest dialogue about your work ethic and your eagerness to succeed at your position.

Don't get me wrong, I'm not asking you to question *every* new work project that comes your way. I am asking you to be realistic about saying "yes" to every new project. Think more clearly about your workload and your ability to successfully complete everything on your plate.

 Ask More Questions!

See what kind of response you receive from your supervisor. Is he or she a rational person? The vast number of rational supervisors I have met would welcome an honest conversation about their employees' workload and work ethic. Sorry, the irrational supervisor will not respond well to this (and might be the subject of a future book!).

It seems we only formally talk about our work ethic at our job interviews, and then only in an abstract way. I believe supervisors more highly regard employees who openly discuss their desire to manage their tasks effectively. Imagine the difference between this type of conversation and the typical, "Why didn't you finish this project?" discussion that is bound to follow your over-committed self.

In our non-work lives I wonder, too, why we don't ask as many questions as we could. Do we too readily accept our life situations without questions? I've met so many people who believe that they can't question systems already in place in their home life. Have you set yourself up for unhappiness because you are afraid to ask for a change? You miss a chance to help your family see that being part of a family means sharing responsibilities. You deny your family your whole, healthy self because you don't want to ask for the needed changes.

Do you think that you have to be a SUPERHERO?

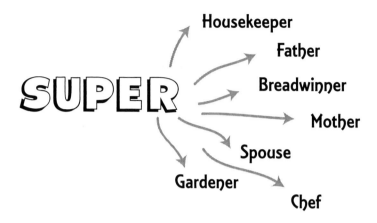

Excelling in any one of these areas is great. However, many people believe that they have to be excellent at everything to confirm their self-esteem and self-worth.

Superheroes, Superman, Spiderman, and Wonder Woman exist in our world as paper and ink drawings, not as a mirror of real life. Yet, many of you reading this book right now are nodding your heads in agreement that you expect yourself to be a Superhero.

Choose to see yourself as a human being—flesh and blood, rather than paper and ink. This choice paves your road to thriving success.

Ask different questions about how you want to live your life. Do you want the debt of a new car—or could an older, reconditioned model serve the same purpose without a huge car payment? Should your children be involved in six different activities or could they be limited to two or three that they enjoy and that would lessen your scheduling dilemmas?

Can the housework, yard work, cooking and laundry chores be redistributed to include more family participation? Can your time be reworked to help you incorporate a bit of exercise or socializing with friends into your schedule?

All of the suggestions in this book will provide you with a bit of respite from your chaos, but all require you to ask different questions or to ask these questions with more conviction.

ASK MORE QUESTIONS!

Ask For Help

Many of you will skip over this section entirely. You (mistakenly) believe that asking for help makes you look weak. That somehow your "star is dimmed" when you ask others to help. Those who continue reading this will likely think, "I've told them that I'm overworked. Can't they see I need

help?" Or, "I've been complaining for weeks about my situation, but no one has stepped up to help."

Perhaps, our American forebearers are to blame for this. The rugged self-reliant nature of those who created our American culture has certainly set a high standard for us to attain. While we have lots to thank these folks for, my personal beef with them involves this issue of self-reliance.

Maybe we've just taken the concept a bit too far. After all, didn't our ancestors gather to raise barns or donate food and clothing to folks who'd fallen on tough times? I wonder if these acts of kindness came with the double-

"The press of full-time work and worrying about two aging and ill parents is enough to make me crazy. I've coped by knowing I can't do this myself and accepting help when it is offered."

Dr. Michelle Emmett, Assistant Vice President for Student Services, Northern Illinois University

edged sword of scorn for the unfortunates who were unable to manage their lives.

No matter. As our culture has evolved, asking for help is seen as a personal weakness. In our work lives we are expected to get all of our work done by ourselves. To speak to our supervisor about getting help from a co-worker might result in demotion or termination. After all, there is always someone else who can handle the workload without help and without comment!

It is also repeatedly expressed to me that employees don't want to "burden their co-workers" with their work as "they have enough to do themselves." If you believe my arguments about the pace of the world and read about the downsizing of business and industry, your logical brain will tell you that we should endlessly and fearlessly be asking for more help. Keep these things in mind as you learn to successfully ask for help.

✓ Be Clear in Your Request

✓ Use a Respectful Tone

✓ Provide the Scope and Rationale for the Help

✓ Outline Expected Outcomes

✻ Be Clear in your Request

Let's return to the thriving activity and our SUPERSTAR holding all of the items. What surprises me most is that the volunteer generally expresses her discomfort, mumbling a little bit about her arms hurting, but seldom ever says "Tracy, I'm overwhelmed here and could use some help."

Remember, the workplace and your home life are fast-paced, chaotic places with many messages competing for attention. Be clear with your requests. I often liken communication today to the old Charlie Brown cartoon specials. When adults talk to Charlie and the gang what the kids hear is "Wa wa wa wa wa wa wa wa." When you are not clear and direct in stating your needs to co-workers, supervisors or family members, you might as well be saying "wa wa wa wa wa wa wa wa."

✻ Use a Respectful Tone

Waiting until you are overwhelmed and very emotional is not going to win allies or assure your supervisor of your competence. Yet, who among us hasn't reached a breaking point where we finally screamed or cried in frustration? My sincerest suggestion is to become comfortable asking for help in a "non-crisis" mode.

Use your logical, rational mind to request help BEFORE a crisis happens. When addressing your supervisor or co-workers, use an assertive tone and "I" statements to clearly express your needs. For instance, "I am totally overwhelmed with this project this afternoon. I need to have someone answer the phone for me for two hours." You may be surprised at the positive reaction this creates.

✳ Provide the Scope of and Rationale for Help

Often, when my volunteer finally can't stand it—or has figured out that he or she can ask for help, people rush in and start grabbing things to relieve the burden. It happens nearly without exception that others remove most of the objects with little thought to the impact of this on the SUPERSTAR.

Imagine being stripped of all responsibility when, in fact, being relieved of one or two particularly cumbersome items might have been enough. Only one time have I ever had an audience member ask the SUPERSTAR which item(s) to take.

When you communicate your needs directly and respectfully, you can also indicate exactly what kind of help you need and for how long you will need it. You shouldn't be relieved of all of your duties indefinitely if you just need one person to help finish binding the report while you create the distribution labels. Your ego is at play here as well. Defining the scope of the help and the rationale in a clear, respectful way helps you to feel more in control.

✳ Outline Expected Outcomes

"If you help me do (X), I will have more time to do (Y)!" If you help me prioritize my work, I will be better able to complete your next major project. If three of us team up on this project, we will get it done two hours quicker than if one of us did it alone. Make sure that your supervisor or co-workers know exactly why the help is necessary and that there are tangible benefits for everyone.

> **THRIVING TIP:**
> Find one project that would make you happy to share— then ask someone for help!

Clearly express the outcomes!

"Okay, Tracy, that makes sense at work, but what about at home?" These four principles also hold true in your home life. Host a family meeting or take your spouse to a quiet dinner to discuss your needs. The tendency to complain without being truly heard is more frustrating than the work you need help with. Be respectful. For instance, continuing to yell at your children to pick up their clothes will net you fewer results than if you catch them off guard with a quiet tone of voice and a specific request.

Offer to Help Others

We've all asked, "Can I help you?" to a friend, spouse or co-worker. Most predictably we receive the, "No thanks, I've got it" answer. We say "okay" and heave a small sigh of relief while continuing on our way. It's a nice routine—

as familiar as Abbott and Costello's "Who's on First?" comedy routine. We offer the help, it's politely declined, and we leave feeling good that we asked, and better that they declined.

We have the same routine in my family. When mom offers to buy me lunch I say, "Oh, no, you shouldn't, let me." To which she says, "I insist." I try again, and she, again, insists. It goes three rounds and only three rounds or else I find myself buying lunch. We each know our respective roles and try not to vary from the script. She feels great treating me to lunch, and I feel great that I tried to buy lunch (but better that she did!).

My mom can buy me lunch, and Bud Costello knows "Who" is actually on first base, but our friends, spouses and coworkers really do need help, even if they play their part to rave reviews by declining our requests.

When you see others who need help and offer to help them, expect them to decline. It's part of our nature to be self-reliant. That's why we don't ask for help. Remember!

Don't take that first decline as the end of the subject. Offer to help on a specific part of a project or offer to answer the phones while your coworker

THRIVING TIP:
Offer your nearest coworker a bit of help. Enjoy his smile!

concentrates on a project. At home you can offer to fold just the towels in a big basket of clothes. Offering something specific increases the chances that you might get her attention in a different way and that she might be more responsive to your offer.

If you still get a "No thanks," after being specific, wait for another opportunity to ask. Sometimes, a repeated request seems more genuine, and the trust in your offer becomes more real. Reassure the other party that it would not be a burden to help and that you have the competence to accomplish what you offer.

Many people decline help from others because they don't think the work will be done correctly and that they'll have to redo it anyway. Anticipate this. Do your best to reassure your coworker that it would not be a burden to help and that you have the competence to accomplish what you offer. Become an expert at offering help.

Develop Systems to Help You Manage the Chaos

Modern technology has made it fun to organize your information, activities, meetings, music and more. Many retail companies offer "systems" to manage your closets, your home office, your kitchen supplies, and just about every aspect of your lives.

When it comes to organizing systems, what I know for sure is that one system does not fit all. What does work for everyone, however, is knowing your particular operational style and building your systems around it.

THRIVING TIP:
Experiment with your friends' organizing systems before investing in your own to see which one will be most effective for you.

Are you a list maker? Do you love crossing things off as you go? Or are you a sticky note person who likes brief reminders placed around you to help you remember and accomplish your goals? Whichever you are, pick a few key organizing tactics that align with your style. And then implement them!

Often there are systems or resources available to us that we fail to notice during our hectic lives. During the SUPERSTAR demonstration, one of the most interesting things that we notice is that amidst the items the SUPERSTAR holds are no fewer than six bags that could be used to hold lots of the other items. The volunteers usually fail to realize this because they become overwhelmed with the enormity of the task and the fast pace in which it is assigned.

Veronica Riepe Director of Student Activities, St. Ambrose College, IA

"My life is made chaotic by the expectations placed on me as well as the expectations I place on myself. I cope by trying to stay organized, realistic, and remember that much of the chaos is really not as important as I may think."

What systems or resources are available to you that you have been too busy to incorporate into your life? Is there a person in your work or personal life who is eager to participate, but is currently underutilized? Have you always done one particular task that could be delegated to others? Do your children have a favorite aunt who would like them to visit more? Let her have them! (Hint, hint, *Elizabeth, Andrew, Kevin, Ian, Alex, Cary, Siobhan, Kelly, Greg, Stephanie, Samantha, Katie, Robby Tiffany, Julia and Sam*)*

Is your neighbor's son old enough to cut your lawn? Hire him! Do you have a new PDA but no time to learn how to use it? Make the time—you'll save it at a later date once it's up and running. Identify and then use those resources readily available!

Take Time for Reflection

As we transition from "systems" thinking, I'd like you to close the book for two minutes and review the systems you have used to manage your day so far. Set a timer so you know when to open the book again!

gratuitous inclusion of author's "children!"

Welcome Back!
You did take a two-minute break didn't you?

If you did use the two minutes to reflect on your current systems, you might be congratulating yourself on your progress thus far; or you might have thought of a way to "tweak" the system so it might be more effective for you.

My guess is that over 50 percent of you did not take the break, or if you did, it was to get a snack or use the restroom. Both good ideas to be sure, but they also prove my point.

We don't take time to reflect.

One of the most important ways for you to thrive in your chaos is to become great at the two-minute reflection. Two minutes is just enough time to contemplate your life without boring yourself or making you unduly uncomfortable.

Audiences generally agree with me that if we had given the SUPERSTAR two minutes and asked her to figure out a way to hold all of the items for 10-15 minutes, she would be more likely to succeed. I think that if I gave the volunteer only 90 seconds, she would still have more success. She would realize her additional resources, would ask good questions, and might even ask for some help.

It seems, however, that we like to jump right into any project that we have without taking a couple of minutes to reflect on what we will be doing. I know from talking to hundreds of audience members that we don't take those reflective moments at the end of the project either. We simply finish up and move right on to the next important thing.

I'm not asking you to enter a Zen-like trance during these reflective moments. I am asking you to take two minutes of quiet time to gain some perspective. Take those moments to plan, brainstorm, prioritize, make a list or just refocus.

> **THRIVING TIP:**
> Invest in a watch with a timer to set the time for your two-minute reflection.

In the office, close the door for two minutes. No door, go to the restroom and sit in a stall! Take a quick walk outside to clear your head and prepare for the next project.

At home—use the travel time between work and home (both ways) to reflect. Turn off the radio. The bathroom might work at home, as will the tub or a quick walk out for the mail.

However you manage it, once you are in the habit of taking these two-minute reflective breaks, you will be amazed at your ability to focus and what you will be able to accomplish. In the words of that modern day philosopher—Dr. Seuss, "*Oh, the thinks you can think!*"

Set Limits on Your Time and Activities

In a world as interesting as ours, it's easy to let our interests and passions overwhelm us. Many years ago, a professional colleague and mentor of mine, Dr. Sara Boatman, wrote a phrase that clearly explains this concept: "Too much of a good thing is still too much."[15] Due to a medical malady she learned this lesson the hard way and shared her insights with others when she was fully recovered. Whether it is chocolate cake you love or volunteering for your favorite organization, you must set some limits. After all, one (large) piece of cake is good; but eating the whole thing is too much.

Chaos does not always stem from negative circumstances. Often, we bring chaos into our lives by the things we love. Maybe you coach your daughter's soccer team and chair a committee for the PTA. Perhaps you offered to write the newsletter for your church, and baked cookies for a bake sale and then offered to update the e-mail addresses of your college friends for the directory, and on, and on, and on. Pretty soon you have taken on too much and feel overwhelmed by the work. You are not able to enjoy any of it.

Each activity, taken separately, might be fun and energizing. You love your daughter and want her to have fun in soccer. You are committed to the PTA's goals and vision. You want your fellow congregants to know what's happening this month. You

> **THRIVING TIP:**
> If you dread going to a meeting or some volunteer activity - resign! Find another way to support the group.

love experimenting with new recipes. Your college friends continue to be important to you. Yet, when these activities are undertaken all together, we see that your best intentions may soon morph into a long and dreaded to-do list.

In your eagerness to please everyone, you might take on too much, thus creating more chaos. Set limits on favors, carpools, kids' activities, as well as the projects you accept at work. Be the person who is very confident in saying, "I'm sorry, I just can't do that for you." Don't give long-winded reasons why. Be firm and consistent. Others will get the message and find someone else to help them.

Set some limits on the extra tasks and projects you allow into your life. Many people endure much more chaos than they should because they want to be involved in everything they are passionate about.

> *"I think those of us who thrive in chaos, live every moment to the fullest. We squeeze everything into our time, whether it's another sport, painting a room, taking on another project, or a hike or vacation. We do whatever it is to fill our time to the fullest."*
>
> Wendy Mackey, Pediatric Nurse Practitioner and mother of three busy kids

Keep Your Eye on the Prize!

"Show me the money!" Remember this famous line from the movie *Jerry Maguire*? Is this your personal motto, "I work hard. Show me the money!"

Do you work for the money alone? I don't think so. Is the money nice? Oh, yeah! Do most of us deserve more than we currently make? You betcha! But is it all about the money? Not a chance!

I like to work. There is something about it that has always felt good to me. I've had many jobs. Some I've liked more than others. And while I enjoy taking time off as much as anyone, I like to work!

All of my jobs have had a high-chaos quotient, each having lots of things out of my control that directly affected my ability to be successful. And, of course, over the years I've brought more chaos into my life through volunteering and maintaining a very active social life. As I review my work history, I am convinced that I gave 110 percent. So convinced, in fact, that I can identify several key points that demonstrate how hard I worked. They include:

☆ **a huge expenditure of physical energy**

☆ **an even greater expenditure of mental energy**

☆ **significant time away from my home and loved ones**

☆ **a true commitment to the organization's values and vision**

☆ **some of my own money**

☆ **a passion and joy for the work**

☆ **willing acceptance of additional responsibilities**

This list looks impressive, don't you think? I continue to give much to my work. But it's not a one-way street. The longer I work, the more I realize that this working relationship brings me many things that I no longer can live without.

Here's the list of the things I feel I receive from my work:

☆ **a profound sense of accomplishment**

☆ **ego fulfillment**

☆ **a commitment to lifelong learning**

☆ **an opportunity to meet great people**

☆ **a creative outlet for my energies**

☆ **an enjoyable staff of fun people**

☆ **time off when I need it**

☆ **money**

☆ **frequent flyer miles**

☆ **opportunities for full engagement**

☆ **friends around the country**

☆ **a happy heart because I know the work I do is important**

☆ **interesting stories about people and places to tell friends and family**

For the privilege of these gifts, however, I am offered the following:

> ☆ **an erratic sleep schedule**
> ☆ **bad eating habits**
> ☆ **less time at home**
> ☆ **time away from those I love**
> ☆ **time away from my dog**
> ☆ **time away from my lake**
> ☆ **lumpy hotel mattresses all around the country**
> ☆ **missing impromptu family and neighborhood gatherings**

Am I willing to continue this chaotic life for just the money? No way! I choose this life. I feel the power in my choice. I do it for the right reasons, and that makes all the chaos worth it.

However, I believe there are some people reading this book who are not in touch with the true prize in their work life. If you just look at your job as a means for making money, you will be unable to manage the chaos for the long term.

What is the Prize?

In the SUPERSTAR exercise, the volunteer will usually endure the discomfort of the burden for quite a long time. During the facilitation I ask the SUPERSTAR why they hold the items so long. Many times they will say, "Because I want the prize." I ask the audience why they didn't help the SUPERSTAR when she obviously needed it. Invariably I hear someone say, "I didn't want her to lose the prize." I laugh when I hear these two responses because I then ask the all-important question. "What is the prize?" No one can answer that question because I don't generally tell what the prize is. I usually say that it's not money, but nothing else to even hint at it. And no one has ever asked me before the exercise begins what the prize is.

The most important thing about the prize is to identify it up front. I know that I work harder when I know what I am getting in return.

Don't be disdainful of others who might ask what their prize is. For instance, if an applicant asks about the benefits offered during a job interview, don't automatically assume

> **THRIVING TIP:**
> Write a personal and professional mission statement to keep you aligned with your "prize."

he is greedy and write him off. I'd prefer to think of him as someone who knows what he wants. I would be happy to have this insight into his motivation.

What is the prize you receive for living your chaotic life? Identify why you work, why you keep a beautiful lawn, or why you chauffeur your children around town. Answering these questions will keep you focused and help you feel better amidst the chaos.

Seek Balance in Your Life

Can you tell when your body is out of balance? Do your fingers swell when you've eaten too many salty foods? Have you gotten a headache when you haven't eaten for a long time? Our bodies are truly miraculous machines, and they work best when we maintain their natural balance.

The great thing about our body is that it tells us, pretty quickly and dramatically, when it is out of balance. Once we notice the imbalance, we can take steps to alleviate the problem, and bring it back into balance.

Why then, is it so difficult for us to notice when our lives are out of balance? I suppose it has to do with our simply not noticing that anything is amiss. That is, until something dramatic forces us to pay attention.

> *"Every day I try to be good to myself in at least one healthy way—taking time to pray, contacting a friend, or reaching out to someone less fortunate than myself are some methods I've used to bring balance to my life."*
>
> Michelle Emmett, Assistant Vice President for Student Services, Northern Illinois University

Maybe forgetting to pick up your daughter after band practice and receiving a frantic call from her alerts you to the craziness. Perhaps you've been too stubborn to give in to a cold, continuing to work until it turns into bronchitis or pneumonia—eventually keeping you in bed for a week. I could list hundreds of examples of how we allow chaos to interfere with the balance in our lives.

Modern medicine and social culture tell us that we're supposed to:

* **eat a balanced diet**

* **maintain a work/life balance**

* **keep a sleep/waking balance**

* **develop a work/play balance**

* **have a spouse/child/self time balance**

* **create an exercise/rest balance**

I would definitely agree with the need for balance in all of these areas. What I see as the problem is our general lack of attention to our *intentions*. If balance is an issue for you, you must be intentional in creating it.

To eat a balanced diet, you have to shop for the right foods. To maintain a work/life balance, you need to leave work at work and home at home. To have a sleep and waking balance, you must go to bed at a proper time—no matter that your favorite movie is a late night feature.

Let's see intention at work.

If I believe that sleep is important to my life balance then I will record my favorite movie for viewing at a time that makes more sense instead of staying up late and creating chaos by my inevitable fatigue. If I believe that exercise is important to my life balance, I will get up earlier, use my lunch hour, hire a babysitter for the kids, talk my spouse into accompanying me (or to cook dinner instead) and thus create the time for it.

Seek balance in your life and be intentional in creating it.

Thrive. Don't Just Cope

We know that the definition of the word "thrive" is to flourish and grow. It's a word filled with hope and promise in the same way that a warm February day holds the promise of the spring to come. I want to thrive, and I want those around me to as well. I'd like this book to be the catalyst for you to thrive.

In my estimation, thriving is an action verb as well as an adjective. It has both physical and emotional components. I strive to be a healthy, vibrant woman who enjoys life and is not afraid to show it. A woman who is physically and emotionally strong despite the chaos that surrounds me. I want other people to feel the same way. I am a woman on a mission! And better still, I am on track to achieving

> **THRIVING TIP:**
> Place notes in places you will see them regularly to remind you to thrive. Better yet, use the tips in this book as a guide to living a more thriving life.

this goal because many years ago I made the decision to THRIVE!

I didn't decide to *just cope* with whatever life brought my way. I wanted more than to merely get by. I wanted to grow!

Have you made a decision about what to do with your life? How are you going to react to the chaos that is a regular part of your life? Do you want to be "the victim," blaming others or wallowing in self-pity? Do you want to complain about the chaos without ever really doing a thing about it? Or, will you put your nose to the grindstone and get the work done but without any joy or sense of fulfillment?

You can choose to cope with it all, leaving little room for true enjoyment, or you can *thrive*, giving yourself the opportunity to learn, grow strong and be happy. I hope you choose to THRIVE!

Look for "Everyday" Humor

Has the dog ever chewed up your favorite rug and then sat next to it with colored strands of fiber clinging to his teeth and tail wagging? Or has your child ever practiced his ABC's in crayon on your dining room wall, proudly asking you to come and see? Perhaps, your friend has asked you to meet at the mall only to wait for an hour in the wrong location?

In each of these scenarios, you have a choice about how you will react. In some houses, if the dog chewed the rug, it would be sent to its kennel for the night—after, of course, some very forceful words were spoken. In some homes the rug would be discarded with forceful words, as might the dog. But in my house, as in many others, I might grab the camera, snap a picture of my beautiful dog, Bailey, and call the neighbors to come and see. All the while laughing like crazy!

Do I want my dog destroying my home? No. But in this situation, I will follow this thought pattern:

* "Look how cute Bailey looks with those strings hanging out of his mouth."

* "I wonder what I did that caused this odd behavior?"

* "Maybe I didn't give him the bone he likes, or didn't play enough with him today."

* "Maybe I didn't give him the attention a growing puppy needs."

* Finally, I would realize, that when you have a puppy and let him roam the house, something's gonna get chewed!

I know I would choose to enjoy the moment. I just can't resist his cute face, his little wagging tail and his desire to please me. Then I would give him a new toy, and turn the rug so you can't see the chewed spot. Actually, knowing

> **THRIVING TIP:**
> Have lunch with a person who can make you smile.

me, I might leave the chewed spot out for a while 'cause it makes a great story to laugh about with guests.

Humor is a major part of my life. It governs my personal relationships. Who doesn't love to make someone else laugh? It impacts my management style. No matter what the problem is, there is always a light-hearted moment if you look for it. And it most assuredly defines my consulting and presentation style.

Everyday life has many humorous moments if we are open to them. And the chaos that we experience can be disarmed at times with a well-placed comment or wry observation.

How often do you laugh in a day? Do you surround yourself with people who enjoy a good sense of humor? If there aren't any around, take charge of your own sense of humor. Find funny stories or comics that

> *"A good laugh always brings order to my chaos!"*
> Amory Lanciano, Mom

amuse you and create a humor file. When you need a boost, open the file and find a good laugh! Ultimately, spend time with people who make you laugh. Or, at the very least, spend more time with happy and upbeat people than with those who always view the glass as half empty.

Simplify, Simplify, Simplify

One of the quickest ways to learn what you can do without is to move into a smaller house. I refused to get rid of any of my possessions when I moved into my smaller house. For the first two years, I could not use either my garage or basement because they were loaded with things I couldn't part with.

After year three of scraping ice and snow off of my car in the New England winters, I realized I needed my garage for the car. Thus began the nearly seven-year task of sorting and purging so that, ultimately, I have ended up with only the things I love the most surrounding me.

My wardrobe went from two full-size closets into one. My jewelry collection shrank from nearly 100 pairs of earrings to about 10 pairs. My holiday decorations went from 20 plastic storage bins (yes, really, 20 bins!) to eight bins. My antique compact collection shrunk to a single compact, my shoes from 60 pairs to a dozen, (sandals not included). You get the idea!

During the journey of sorting and purging my things, I sorted and purged other areas of my life as well. Worries—gone; people who drain my energy—gone; old perceived conflicts—gone!

What I realized throughout this process, a tough and at times heart-breaking process, is that:

> ### *SIMPLE IS BETTER IN A LIFE THAT IS ALREADY CHAOTIC.*

There were many things I could simplify while still maintaining an abundant level of joy. It felt great to practice what I have been preaching to others!

Simplifying in Action!

I had a client whose office was a mess. Now I can relate to this; it's hereditary in my family, but my client's clutter had so taken over that she had only about eight square inches of true workspace on her desk. It had started to impact her ability to be effective.

One of the most fun and interesting areas of her office included an extensive Koosh ball collection. For those unfamiliar with the Koosh ball, it is a rubbery stringy ball that people play with and use as a stress reducer. The Koosh people have developed what seems like hundreds of different shapes, colors and styles of these adorable toys and my client had nearly all of them. To be fair, this collection added visual interest to the office and was occasionally used by the office occupant and guests. But mostly it just took up space—a lot of space.

One of my first tasks with this client was to help her regain control of her space and develop some systems to help her feel more in control. At first she was adamant that the Koosh collection stay. She felt it only right to display it because so many people had contributed to the collection. Plus, she did have an emotional attachment to the collection.

After working our way around the office, carefully avoiding the Koosh shrine, this client started to feel better about herself and felt the burden of disorganization lift. She eventually gained the courage to tackle the Kooshes.

Before we dismantled them. however, we took digital photographs of them, which could eventually be used as a computer screen saver. We then identified the Kooshes that had the most sentimental value to her and kept those three for her everyday use. We put a couple of them away because she just couldn't part with them, and she distributed the rest of them as gifts to her friends and coworkers.

The former Koosh shrine is now a more useful space. The remaining Kooshes are truly stress-relieving playthings and the office occupant, a much happier and more productive employee.

THRIVING TIP:
Try life without one of your collections for a while. After a month, decide if you still need it. If not, there's always E-Bay! *(Just don't buy anything else!)*

It is a long story on simplification; yet, many of us can't get rid of things we own because of sentimental attachments. Keep as much as you can adequately manage, but pay attention when it becomes too much!

Does your collection need polishing, dusting or constant care? Is more valuable time used caring for it than enjoying it? Is the collection a substitute for something you might be missing in another area of your life? These are good questions for you to ponder. As you do, think too of this. Is there something else you could be doing for yourself if you didn't have all of this "stuff" to manage?

I have mentioned the emotional stuff I began to purge from my life. What could be purged from your life as well?

Take Life-Enhancing Risks!

Are you interested in bungee jumping off a bridge or parachuting from a plane? Not for you? What's the matter? Too risky? Many people report that the risk is worth it, and they felt exhilarated doing it, even those who broke a leg upon landing!

I believe that to thrive in your chaos, you are going to have to take some risks. Not life-threatening risks, but life-enhancing risks. Which, by the way, might feel like the same thing to some folks!

I've heard stories of risk-averse people who refuse to go on a picnic if there's even a chance of rain, and others who won't drive home a different way for fear of excess traffic. I imagine that some who read this book will reject making any changes suggested here because of their fear of change.

Noted business guru, Tom Peters, in his book *The Pursuit of WOW*, has a great quote on change. He says, "It takes forever to maintain change; but it takes just a flash to achieve change of even the most profound sort."[16]

If you've ever dieted and then gained the weight back, you will agree wholeheartedly with Tom. Yet, at least you took the risk of losing the weight. If you let yourself be psyched out by negative thinking (i.e., "I'll probably gain the weight back so what's the use?"), you will lose out on an opportunity to see if you can keep the weight off and be happier with yourself.

Risk is defined by dictionary.com as: *1. exposure to the chance of injury or loss; a hazard or dangerous chance. It's synonyms are, venture, peril, jeopardize, endanger.*[17]

No wonder so many people are risk-averse! Why would we ever want to put ourselves in peril or jeopardy? Even for the chance of a happy or positive outcome. Because if you don't, nothing will ever change!

For example, you might have asked your children two years ago to help by making their beds. When you initially asked them, they were reluctant and did not follow up on your request. From this you learned that the children are resistant to helping, so you don't take the risk of asking them again.

> "If your life lacks at least some element of chaos, you aren't living well!"
>
> Mary Robison,
> Wife/Mom/Teacher/Tutor

I want you to ask them again. I want you to take a different approach this time. I want you to imagine a different outcome from the previous encounter. Strategize the conversation before asking, and develop language to overcome their objections to your request. Develop an alternative task if they are resistant to the first one. Think of a reward that you might have in your "back pocket" to sweeten the deal. In other words, I want you to take a calculated risk that will enhance your life.

What other areas of your life need a life-enhancing risk? Is there a position at work that you would love to have, but have been reluctant to pursue because you weren't sure you were qualified? Take the risk. Is there someone you want to be closer to but haven't made any overtures because you fear some rejection? Take the risk and make contact with that person.

In all cases, do your homework so that you aren't blindly taking risks. This is one of the most important ways you can take "peril and jeopardy" out of the scenario. Find out as much as you can about what the new position might entail and see how your skills align. Find out the interests of the person you want to meet and strike up a conversation using an interesting opening line.

I like to watch people file into the room when I am preparing to present a workshop. Many people get to the room early, not out of a sense of excitement about the learning, but because they want to sit in the seat that they always sit in. For some, this is the front; but for most it's the back row. I watch the careful posturing, the eyes scanning the room to see who is sitting where and with whom. I see them try out a row only to move to a different spot when someone else chooses that row.

THRIVING TIP:
Have coffee with someone different this week. See if you are changed in any way by the experiment.

I have a mean streak! I admit it! After watching 30 minutes of careful seat placement, I invariably conduct an activity that forces people to move into different seats. I love the momentary look of terror that passes their faces when they realize they will have to move.

But more than my enjoyment at their discomfort, I take joy in knowing that they will meet someone during the workshop that might change their lives. They will step out of their comfort zone for a positive purpose and be enhanced because of it. I only wish that it would happen more spontaneously once they leave the workshop setting.

Take a risk that just might change you!

Actual Thriving Tips from Workshop Participants

The previous tips speak to my vision for how you can bring more joy into your chaotic existence. I strongly believe that if you incorporate them into your life, you will be better able to thrive.

At many of the *Thriving in Chaos* workshops I have facilitated, I have asked participants to generate ideas for thriving. The next section includes their ideas and my spin on them. There are thriving tips for both your personal and professional life. Enjoy!

Thriving Tips
Specifically for Your Personal Life

- ❖ Take Time for Yourself
- ❖ Develop a Hobby
- ❖ Laugh a Lot
- ❖ Exercise
- ❖ Own Your Attitude
- ❖ Absolve Yourself of Guilt
- ❖ Be Flexible
- ❖ Volunteer for Something
- ❖ Stop Procrastinating
- ❖ Set Realistic Goals
- ❖ Change What's Not Working
- ❖ Say "No" More Often
- ❖ Be Honest About Your Strengths and Weaknesses
- ❖ Spend Time With Your Friends
- ❖ Get Some Sleep
- ❖ Hire Some Services
- ❖ Take Care of Your Health
- ❖ Celebrate Good Times

❖ Take Time for Yourself

You've heard it a million times. If you take time for yourself, you'll have more to give others. Turns out, there's a reason we hear it so often. It's true!

> *"Drink wine - only good wine - otherwise you add another element of chaos - a hangover!"*
> Page Wallert, Mom

When you put yourself first, for instance, scheduling time to exercise, meditate, and participate in your hobbies, you refresh your body. When you feel better, you are happier and are more willing to give to others. You also have that sense of satisfaction that you don't have to share with anyone!

Taking time for yourself may feel like a guilty pleasure. Especially if you hear your world still revolving outside of your closed bedroom door. Get over the guilt and just focus on the pleasure! It is an investment that will bring you and those around you great rewards.

❖ Develop a Hobby

Do you enjoy going to a craft fair and admiring the wares? Have you thought to yourself, "I could make that myself if I had the time?" Make the time! The positive benefits you will reap from engaging in your hobby will carry over to many aspects of your life.

Many hobbies involve creating something, whether it is woodworking, gardening, jewelry making, knitting or stitching. The relaxation and exhilaration you will experience from the creative process can be a welcome respite to the chaos of everyday life.

Another client of mine has a room lined from floor to ceiling with stamping supplies. She creates the most beautiful cards with them. The compliments she receives for her work give her great satisfaction that is an additional bonus to the sense of calm she feels when she creates the cards. Many others call their hobbies "therapy." No matter the medium you enjoy collecting rare books, growing orchids or watching old movies it's all good for your soul!

✤ Laugh A Lot!

I have already discussed looking for "everyday" humor, but as I write this I am preparing a workshop entitled, *Humor in the Workplace.* Did you know that there are many tangible benefits to laughter? It increases blood flow around the body, gives you a way to release endorphins (or "endolphins" as a friend of mine calls them.) Laughter even exercises many muscles in the body.

Honestly, is there a more perfect place to find humor than at work? Where else can you find such a wide assortment of people with interesting life stories who do crazy, silly or odd things? Look around your workplace. There is probably a lot to laugh about.

I'd say look around your home as well. Have the kids done something that you can choose to laugh at rather than yell about? Look for the humor in your life and, then, don't just grin or chuckle. Laugh out loud! Really give it a go. You'll be surprised at how contagious the laughter is and how truly good you'll feel when you are done.

❖ Exercise

I don't know about you, but I'm patiently waiting for that "exercise high" touted by all the fitness magazines. Over the years, I have been a swimmer, a runner, a walker and a couch potato. My favorite of course, is the "spud!" I've had many a "high" eating a pint of ice cream while watching my favorite movie! Still waiting for it to happen while I am sweating! Having said that, I do know that the sense of accomplishment I feel when I walk two miles or run a bit longer than usual. It is a cool feeling.

To be able to say, "I worked out today," makes me proud. I like "exercising Tracy." How about you? Got all of the excuses down pat about why you don't exercise?

Do this: Exercise for 15 minutes. Not anything too strenuous (and make sure that it meets your doctor's approval.) Write down how it feels to say, "I worked out today." When you evaluate the positive feelings that this exercise engenders, you will realize that the positives outweigh the negatives. Really, the hardest part of any workout is deciding to actually do it!

❖ Own Your Attitude

We've all met those people who never seem to be in a bad mood. What's their secret? Pharmaceuticals? Perhaps! But more likely, they've decided to have infinite control over their attitude.

> "Challenges are opportunities turned around."
>
> Lin Anderson, Senior Director of Physical Education, Middlesex YMCA, Middletown, CT

It's Monday and you are late for a meeting. It's cloudy and rainy. Do you have to be in a bad mood? Does your whole day have to be ruined because of circumstances beyond your control?

I've had women *and* men tell me that they have had "bad hair days" that literally put them in a bad mood all day long. It is a mystery to me why a misplaced lock of hair can cause someone emotional pain.

I think the hair is an excuse for something else going wrong in their lives that they don't want to admit. And I want to believe, that with very few exceptions, we can choose our attitude. Give it a try—vow to be cheerful during the next rainy day!

❖ Absolve Yourself of Guilt

In *Hamlet*, William Shakespeare writes, "My stronger guilt defeats my strong intent."[18] While speaking to women about my Thriving in Chaos book, one of the most recurrent themes became that of guilt. Guilt that you are not dong enough. Guilt that you are not spending enough time with the family. Guilt that you are not doing enough at work or that you haven't worked out enough. This guilt weighs you down. It does not allow you to ever fully enjoy or appreciate all that you do for yourself and others.

If you have broken a law or commandment, or kicked your cat, or done something equally evil, feel guilty. For the rest of you, however, I think you are carrying around too much extra guilt. It is *not* part of your DNA, religious belief or a rite of passage after becoming a mom. The "right" to feel guilty is reserved only for a precious few.

Guilt over things that you have or haven't done or said doesn't really change anything. It actually stops you from learning and growing from the experience. If you honestly have something to feel guilty about you should reflect on what caused it to happen and figure out a way to avoid it in the future. When you *only* feel guilty, you usually obsess about it, using your emotional brain and not your logical one. This makes learning from the experience nearly impossible.

So, how are you going to stop feeling guilt?. You just stop! If these paragraphs have been speaking directly to you, most

> "It's so hard when there is so much going on. It's that little voice in our female heads that keeps telling us that we are not doing 'good enough'. As the layers pile on, I realize that no one means it to happen, I just don't feel able to manage anything!"
>
> Carolyn Didden, Teacher, Mom

likely you are in the habit of feeling guilty over everything. You can retrain your brain to stop obsessing. When you catch yourself feeling guilty, redirect your thoughts to more pleasant things.

Generally, your children will never think they have enough of you. That's part of their childish charm. The house will likely never be clean enough—at least if you lead an interesting life. And, the tasks on your desk at work will probably multiply behind your back. We seldom ever see a blank to-do list.

Become more comfortable believing that you are doing a good job. That you are good to your family. That you are successful. You will be amazed at how good you can feel.

♣ Be Flexible
The ability to adapt has served humanity nearly from the beginning of time. It is our adaptability that allows us to

change and subsequently grow. There are some times when it's in our best interest to be flexible. For instance, when flying.

When an airline has oversold a flight, it will typically ask for passengers with "flexible travel plans" to take a later flight—often for the perk of a round trip ticket. In this case, being flexible provides a windfall. I wonder what other windfalls might occur in our everyday lives if we were more flexible?

Flexibility, adaptability, and ease with change are all concepts that are a must in this chaotic world. And even more than just being flexible, I suggest that you refer back to the previous tips and own a positive rather than a grudging attitude about it. Don't just "hrumpfff" and say, "O-kay, I'll do it." when flexibility is called for. Invite it in like an old friend and then find the good in the experience.

❖ Volunteer for Something

"Oh no, she's asking us to put yet another task on the to-do list!" Well, yes, I guess I am. I'd like you to consider doing some occasional volunteer work. Here's why: If chosen well the volunteer experience will bring many positive benefits into your life. It has the power to center you. It makes you feel good toward others and good about yourself. It has a positive impact on your community. There really is no downside—except for your already overtaxed schedule. So, how are you going to fit it in?

---

* Do you have children in school? Try volunteering in their classroom once a month.

* Develop a family volunteer day once or twice a quarter at the dog pound or at your local animal hospital.

* Contact the local nursing home and ask about reading to a resident or accompanying them on an outing. Volunteers are helpful on these trips.

* Help an elderly neighbor with mowing or gardening.

Be sure to take a bit of time afterward to reflect on the contributions you have made and their impact on others. Your activity doesn't have to have a long-term commitment. But I guarantee that if you find something you love, you'll get a long-term, positive benefit from the experience.

> *"Everyday in my job can be chaos. Today I had the opportunity to participate in the United Way Day of Caring. It was nice to give back to the community in a way that I don't often get to."*
> Cindy Beals, Director of Student Activities, Vincennes University

❖ Stop Procrastinating

I am the WRONG PERSON to be advising this. Yet, I know in my heart, it is a great tip. Let's prove the importance of this tip by looking at our life when we procrastinate.

When given a deadline, most people can find a million reasons not to start the project. Everything else seems more interesting than actually working on it. But just as you are coasting along, suddenly something happens that makes you aware that the deadline is looming. As soon as you realize this:

– **Your heart starts to race.**

– Your adrenaline begins to flow.

– **Your brain kicks into overdrive.**

— You begin frantically searching for all of the information/tools you need to complete the task.

– **You freak out when you realize that the task is MUCH BIGGER than you originally envisioned.**

– You snap at your sweetheart.

– **You get angry and defensive if anyone approaches you about anything else.**

– You are single-minded in getting it done.

– **You are causing chaos, confusion and angst to those around you.**

– You are oblivious to this.

– **You spend many sleepless nights.**

– You deprive yourself of something good and fun with your friends.

– **You complain about this.**

– *Finally,* you finish the project!

Many of you are laughing right now and thinking, "What's the big deal, at least it got done!" And many more of you are thinking, "She nailed it! It's pure torture to be with this procrastinator."

Folks, the negatives outweigh the positives here. In a world out of control, this is one of the <u>only things</u> you can control. **Stop procrastinating! DO IT NOW!**

❖ Set Realistic Goals

I will lose ten pounds by next week. I will run five miles by Tuesday. I will have that 60-page report ready for you in one week. My child will go to Yale. My dog will win the National Dog Show.

Please begin humming "The Impossible Dream" from *The Man from LaMancha* right now!

It is our nature to want to succeed and succeed fast. It has also become our nature that when we don't succeed, we no longer "try, try again." We usually give up.

The reason so many people give up their goals is because they fail to set reasonable ones. When we set reasonable goals and develop a plan to achieve them, we stand a far greater chance for success. Lots of small successes beat a large failure every time. Decide to lose two pounds next week. Run one-quarter mile by Tuesday and have 20 pages of your report ready by next week. Help your child have a great day at pre-school and take your dog to an obedience class. Let's start small and work our way up.

❖ Change What's Not Working

Complaining is fun. That MUST be why so many people do it. We all know people who complain about things in their work or personal lives.

> *"Each year I think 'my life cannot get any more chaotic' and each year it does!"*
> Leslie Heusted, Director of Student Life and Development, Maryville University of St. Louis

What happens when you try to give these complainers some good advice on solving their problems? They typically get angry and defensive, lashing out that "you just don't understand." Trouble is, you understand all too well. Many people refuse to change something that's not working.

It's much more fun to complain about a poor relationship with a co-worker than to actively work to repair the relationship. It's much easier to express frustration with your child's messy room than come up with a series of rewards for the desired behavior.

Dr. Phil McGraw, noted TV advice guru, has a line about these complainers that I like. He says, "How's that working for you?" He realizes that some people are chronic complainers and that they "get something" out of the complaining.

Listening to complainers is tiresome. Listening to someone speak about changing something they used to complain about is inspiring!

Let's not hold on to old systems "just because." Let's figure out what's not working and change it in a way that makes life easier.

❖ Say "No" More Often

It's a two-letter word that is treated like a 4 letter word. It's scary to some, intimidating to others. NO, no, no, no, no, no, no and no. Let me help you with this. Here are 14 ways for you to say "No".

"No, but I'll write a check."

"No thank you."

"No, it's not the right time."

"No, I'm flattered you asked."

"No, but ask me again in three weeks."

"No, I'm sure there's someone just as qualified."

"No, but maybe John can do it."

"NO, I NEED A BREAK."

"No, but I'll develop an outline so Peggy can follow it."

"No, I'm too overwhelmed right now."

"No"

"No, but how wonderful of you to think of me."

"No, not right now."

"No, my kids and spouse need my full attention right now."

Steal mine, or invent your own. The art of saying "no" is really the art of taking control of your life. The ability to do this gracefully will help reduce the guilt you feel at having to say "no."

Beware! Those asking are tricky. They want you! Resist their flattery: "Come on Tanya, you are the best at this." Resist their guilt: "Donald, if you don't do this the children will suffer." Resist their sniping: "*Well*, Ducky is helping. It's the least you can do."

If it doesn't fit into your plans, whatever **IT** is, just say "no!"

❖ Be Honest About Your Strengths and Weaknesses

I've heard of people who never look at themselves in a full- length mirror. I wonder what they are trying to hide?

On the television show *"What Not to Wear,"* in an effort to have the participant fully understand her fashion faux pas, she is put into a 360-degree mirror. After this experience the participant realizes the errors of her fashion ways and becomes more amenable to the hosts' clothing suggestions.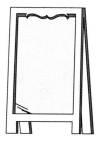

I wish there were a 360-degree mirror that would reveal what's inside of us! Something that would help us see our strengths and weaknesses very clearly and make us more amenable to the necessary corrections.

It is not always easy to face the truth about either your strengths or weaknesses. But it is absolutely necessary in order for you to be able to anticipate chaos-creating behaviors and correct them as needed.

If you know that you are disorganized and accept this about yourself, you can avoid the inevitable chaos when it's time to go somewhere by starting out 10 minutes earlier to look for your keys. I'm not asking you to be *more organized.* Just to add a bit more time in your schedule to accommodate the "scramble" to find the keys.

In the workplace, knowing your strengths and weaknesses can help you in hiring people to complement your skill-set or create a great work team. It can also allow you to have more meaningful conversations about your work or workload with your supervisor.

Don't bury your head in the sand. Face yourself in the mirror and see who you truly are!

❖ Let the "Spirit" Move You

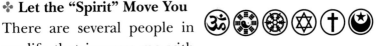

There are several people in my life that impress me with their spirituality. They don't just "go through the motions" of attending religious services. They truly embrace their spirituality and use their faith as a way to center themselves. When I speak with any of them about their faith, I feel better. I know their faith makes a world of difference to them.

It's not my job to talk you into joining a church or going to services. However, I do think that it's my job to help you see that others gain quite a bit of calm by embracing their faith or living a spiritual life.

If you have a church home, allow the peace you feel there to follow you to your home. Make a habit of reflecting or praying when the chaos gets to be too much for you. For those who do not have a church home, many people identify their spirituality with nature. Take some time to fully appreciate the beauty of the world around you.

Perhaps reading some of the great philosophers or modern day spiritualists will help you gain personal peace. If that doesn't seem like a good fit for you, simply taking a few quiet moments to yourself may help you to find an inner peace. When you are regularly in touch with your spirit, you are much more able to get through the crazy chaos of your life.

❖ Spend Time With Your Friends

The television show *"Friends"* had a very successful ten-year run. The idea of six very different people sharing their lives was very appealing to the television audience.

I can't help thinking that what we envied most about this series is not the fact that they were friends; but, rather, how much time they spent with each other. They were always sipping coffee together at Central Perk or eating Monica's cooking at the apartment that everyone lived in

> *"This year chaos bumped into me through the experiences of my sister and several friends. I worked hard to be supportive of them, while acknowledging that their chaos was now a part of me, too."*
> Karen Anderson, Director of Resident Services, Whitney Center

at one time or another. They were allowed to just hang out. Think how much better your life could be if you could just hang out more with your friends. Friends are precious. They have been hand picked by you to provide exactly what you need.

Have you noticed however, how difficult it is to schedule time with your friends? It seems everyone's life has gotten busier. Time with our friends is a luxury now. One that I say—indulge in! You need your friends to help you weather life's challenges. Your friends gather round during the big events: births, deaths, marriage, divorce. We depend on their strength to sustain us.

Fortunately, life is not just filled with big events. It has small, amazing and annoying ones too! Make the time to see your friends and let them work their magic on you during these little times too.

❖ Get Some Sleep

I already know what my platform would be if I were selected as Miss America. (Don't snicker!) I would passionately lobby for people to get more sleep. I would extol the virtues of a good night's sleep at every promotional stop, while proudly wearing my tiara! (And maybe even my pajamas!)

Sleep is an important part of living, even though that sounds like a contradiction of terms. Our *sleep hours* help make our *waking hours* more interesting, pleasant and productive. There is almost no problem that doesn't "look better in the morning." *We* even look better in the morning after a good night's sleep.

Sleep has recuperative powers that are both physical and emotional. When we give our bodies the necessary amount of sleep (for most people that is 7-8 hours), we create an opportunity for our body to renew itself. Don't believe me? Ever see a three-year-old who has missed his nap? He is cranky, tearful, obstinate, prone to tantrums, and unable to concentrate. In other words, not very pleasant to be around! I don't know how old you are as you read this; but I'd wager that when you don't get enough sleep, we see these traits from you too!

> *"My favorite day out of the year falls whenever we get to fall back an hour - daylight savings time. Any day that I can pick-up an extra hour is a great day for me."*
> Ken Brill, Associate Dean of Students, Augustana College

Make sleep a priority. According to the National Sleep Foundation, it will increase your ability to: stay healthy, concentrate, keep your patience, juggle multiple tasks, and feel good about yourself.[19] These skills are essential in your quest to thrive in your chaos. Don't skimp on your sleep.

✤ Hire Some Services

The business world is becoming very comfortable paying for certain services that others can provide more efficiently and cost effectively. "Outsourcing" has become a business buzzword as well as a new millennial management practice. Why don't more families embrace this outsourcing philosophy to more efficiently and effectively manage their homes?

There has been an explosion of services available to help working families accomplish their household chores. You can hire:

❏ House cleaners	❏ Personal clothes shoppers
❏ Dog walkers	❏ Grocery delivery
❏ Yard crews	❏ Drivers for the elderly

And, according to Craigslist.com, you can also hire a hairdresser on wheels, birthday party planners (including baking the cake and filling the goody bags) a vegan personal chef, or a sister-duo to paint a mural on your child's bedroom wall! Those sound like fun!

I realize that these services cost money. However, could you find a way to justify the expense by placing a higher value on what you gain from being freed from the task yourself?

I will never forget the look on my sister, Amory's, face when she walked into her house after the first time a cleaning crew had worked their magic. I'd like to bottle the joy and relief she felt! It was a great burden lifted. I think she would have paid double to feel that way again. And the good news continued. Her boys, Andrew and Kevin, noticed and made an effort (as much as any 11 and 8-year-old will make) to keep it clean.

You will feel the same way when your lawn is mowed or the groceries are delivered to your door. That feeling is worth something. See if there is a way you can outsource a job or two. Then, pay attention to how it allows you to thrive in some other area of your life.

> *"One of the best ways to combat chaos is to sit down in a comfy chair, with a cup of tea, and a book about thriving in it. Oh, and send the kids off on a long, impossible trip to the grocery store with Dad."*
>
> Irene Liebler, Wearer of many hats

✤ Take Care of Your Health

Ouch! As you are chewing your tofu burger, you notice that a tooth is a bit sensitive. Oh well, you think, "I'll just chew on the other side!" Two weeks later, on your vacation in Disney World, that tooth becomes infected, causing you to miss a full day in the sun finding a dentist and having an emergency root canal.

Does this example ring true for you? I can't tell you the number of times I have put off "routine" medical procedures because I was "too busy" or didn't hurt enough to make a big deal out of it. Usually, I am okay, but there have been several notable examples of this backfiring on me. And an emergency root canal is only fun for the dentist!

Let's be honest, nobody really enjoys a health tune up. It is just something you have to do. Many of us have well-developed systems for avoiding boring or routine things. However, lately I have seen too many lives disrupted for health related reasons, causing unspeakable chaos. It's time to put yourself first.

Our automobiles come with a manual that clearly explains the routine maintenance that will keep them working at optimal levels. With our bodies there are no owners guides—except for the recommendations of various health care agencies. But we do know the basics.

1. **Have an annual check up.**
2. **Perform skin and breast checks to look for changes.**
3. **For men, have your PSA levels checked.**
4. **Have regular mammograms.**
5. **Visit the dentist for good oral hygiene.**
6. **Pay attention to changes in your body, how it feels, and operates. Alert your healthcare professional to something that doesn't seem right.**
7. **Eat foods that are good for you more often than not.**
8. **Sneak a bit of physical activity into your everyday routine.**

Reduce the amount of chaos for yourself and others by taking good, pro-active, care of your health!

❖ "Celebrate Good Times—Come On!"

Kool and the Gang were on to something! They sang this song, which became an instant classic. This song could be one of my personal theme songs. I love to celebrate! Usually, I don't need a reason—"It's Tuesday, let's celebrate!"

I come by this honestly. I grew up in a family where celebration was revered. My parents were great hosts and taught us kids to appreciate a celebration. Our house was decorated for every holiday. Our birthdays were special events. Perhaps that's why, in the early part of my professional career, I was a program planner.

To emphasize celebrating is *not just* to emphasize partying. I think we should be more celebratory in all areas of our life. I think we should celebrate the end of a big project at work, instead of just moving on to the next project. I think we should celebrate the big and small transitions in our home life too.

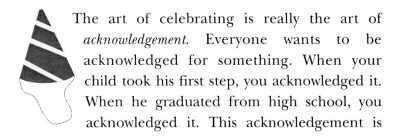

The art of celebrating is really the art of *acknowledgement*. Everyone wants to be acknowledged for something. When your child took his first step, you acknowledged it. When he graduated from high school, you acknowledged it. This acknowledgement is ego boosting and motivating. It is recognition of great effort and its eventual results.

We typically celebrate big events. But I am going to ask you to celebrate your small victories too. Maybe you stood up for yourself to your supervisor and got a new policy changed. Good for you! Celebrate being assertive and smart. Maybe you expressed your opinion at a meeting where you usually felt intimidated. Celebrate this change in your behavior. Perhaps, you tried a new recipe and the family loved it. Celebrate the joy in your accomplishment.

> "As a working mom of five kids, a wife and a daughter, I would just love to have a sense of accomplishment at the end of the day."
>
> Lori Roche, Tracy's Hero!

When you don't celebrate, either because you are too busy, or the accomplishment does not seem worthy of a true celebration, you deny yourself an affirming opportunity. You may feel that your extra efforts are for naught. This feeling robs you of some potential and deserved joy. It does nothing to help you stay motivated for all that faces you.

Pick a couple of ways that you can celebrate your own accomplishments. It doesn't need to involve fancy napkins or invitations. It might be as simple as having a glass of wine when you get home or treating yourself to a new bestseller. Whatever you decide to try, make sure that you know what you did to deserve it!

Thriving Tips
Specifically for Your Professional Life

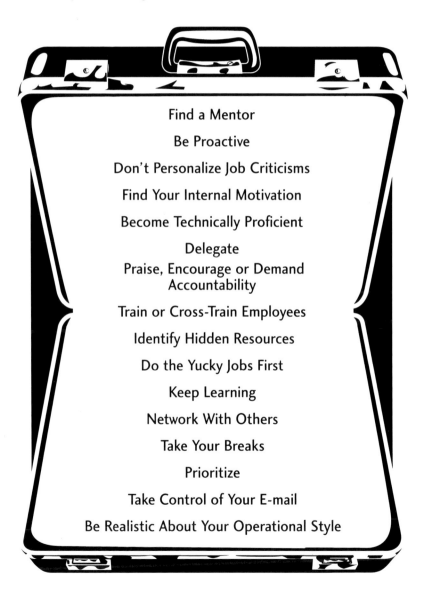

Find a Mentor

Be Proactive

Don't Personalize Job Criticisms

Find Your Internal Motivation

Become Technically Proficient

Delegate

Praise, Encourage or Demand
Accountability

Train or Cross-Train Employees

Identify Hidden Resources

Do the Yucky Jobs First

Keep Learning

Network With Others

Take Your Breaks

Prioritize

Take Control of Your E-mail

Be Realistic About Your Operational Style

✝ Find a Mentor

From nearly the beginning of civilization, young men and later, women, were taught a trade through the practice of apprenticeships. They were sent to an artisan, craftsman, or tradesman to be taught all the intricacies of their particular field.

Nowadays, there are only a few professions that still incorporate apprenticeship as a formal teaching method. But it seems to me that this technique is where our modern day mentoring programs came from.

A mentor is someone who has taken on the role of informal teacher and guide: a person who wants you to succeed and has committed a bit of his or her time and effort to see that it happens. The mentor gets the satisfaction of watching you explore, learn, and grow. He or she gets to feel a bit of success with each of your successes.

A mentor is someone who:

> ✓ has a work ethic you respect and may emulate
>
> ✓ you can speak honestly with
>
> ✓ is in you corner, rooting for your success
>
> ✓ you can bounce ideas off of in a safe and supportive environment
>
> ✓ will help shoulder the burden of your work
>
> ✓ can help you quickly learn the culture of your organization and its policies

Some companies offer a formal mentoring program where you are paired up with another person. If offered, take advantage of this opportunity. If it's not offered, look around your company to find someone you respect. Ask them if you can establish an informal mentoring relationship. Your job performance will be enhanced and your work experience will be heightened if you have a willing and experienced hand to guide you.

> *"I've worked in college student activities for 29 years. Attempting to serve as a role model for students just starting to learn time/life management skills is a constant challenge in this ever expanding world."*
>
> Meri Phillips, Director of Student Activities, College of DuPage, IL

✢ Be Proactive

This sounds like a no-brainer. "Yeah, Tracy, be proactive." If it is so self-evident, why don't more people practice it?

I think it's hard to be proactive, to think ahead, anticipate, or plan because we are so busy doing things. When you are in "get 'er done" mode, you don't want to stop for a time out. You think you'll lose momentum. But I am here to assure you that you will never go wrong taking a minute to plan. Previously I spoke of the two-minute reflection. This technique will help you see what needs to be done and give you time to develop a plan to accomplish your work.

Being proactive will also help you think through the consequences of your actions or inaction.

For instance, many of you send e-mails to others in your company. Have you ever neglected to copy someone in on an e-mail, only to receive a hostile e-mail from him or her later in the day? Now you have hurt feelings and a relationship to repair. This extra burden takes time away from your already busy day.

Try taking another minute or two before you take actions at work. Implement the two-minute reflection. In other words, think before you act. It's a sure-fire way to reduce some of the action-induced chaos you bring upon yourself.

✛ Don't Personalize Job Criticisms

Nobody likes to be criticized. Yet, nobody is perfect. Don't we all think that we do a good job at work? We feel that we put forth a strong effort, we do our best, and this should be good enough. Alas, sometimes it's not! Everyone deserves some criticisms (or "coaching" as we call it in the new millennium).

Yet, if you do not acknowledge this fact, you may internalize the criticism and become extremely emotional about it. When you are emotional, you are not focused on your work. And of course, you simply must tell your co-workers about how you were criticized by the boss.

We all can improve our work. Even pilots and brain surgeons—who *have* to do a good job *every time*—must learn new techniques that will make them more effective. Don't let your ego get in the way of progress. Take the criticisms for what they are worth. Decide what you can change and then move on. You will feel better and, maybe, perform better too!

✢ Find Your Internal Motivation

Many people call me a motivational speaker. I don't call myself that, even though I know people are sometimes moved by what I say. Am I just being modest? Heck no! It's just that I realized a long time ago a very simple concept.

People motivate themselves.

I cannot motivate anyone to do anything. It all comes from within each of us.

In my twenty plus years of consulting experience, I have found that there are some common things that motivate us all.

1. Being given a chance to learn and grow.

2. Being recognized for our work.

3. Feeling that our work makes a difference.

4. Knowing that our opinions are valued.

5. Feeling that we belong.

6. Enjoying our co-workers and having fun.

Notice, I didn't put money on the list. Studies, too numerous to list, have indicated that very few of us are truly motivated by the money we make.

So, which of thesemotivates you the most in your job? Right now, I am most motivated by recognition from others and knowing that my work makes a difference. In other jobs, I have been more motivated by opportunities to learn and grow and have fun. Once you can identify your internal motivation, you can create an environment where you will get what you want out of your work.

> "My motto is work hard, play harder... I work so I can live my life to its fullest."
> Dr. Lucy Croft
> Assistant Vice President for Student Affairs University of North Florida

✤ Become Technically Proficient

When I worked in a professional office everyday, I became the "copy machine queen." I could troubleshoot nearly any problem and prided myself on this ability. There wasn't a paper jam I couldn't fix!

Back then, my working knowledge of several computer programs and lots of speedy ways to get things done was unrivaled.

However, since I have not worked in an office for many years now, I feel technology passing me by. Copy machines of today are more digital than manual. I wouldn't even know where to turn it on! And I'm sure that my laptop can do things I haven't dreamed of, but there is nobody at the desk next to mine showing me how to create a shortcut or teaching me about the latest fonts.

Technology and all that it can do has exploded in the last 15 years. Are you keeping up? Many of you who work with lots of co-workers have a ready supply of teachers willing to show you ways to be more efficient. Nevertheless, some of you still won't learn the new tricks of the trade.

I already discussed our fear of change. I gave you some suggestions to help you overcome this fear. Implement them here! Make peace with technology and let it help you reduce your chaos.

✛ Delegate

As the SUPERSTAR shows us time and again, we think, or like to think, that we can do it all. We will hold whatever load is given, and then add even more to it. We will suffer in silence trying to juggle everything until we drop it all.

Just as I said we treat "no" as if it were a four-letter word, I think we bestow the same honor to the eight-letter word DELEGATE. Most people are reluctant to delegate. Many people are actually afraid to delegate.

Here's why:

> 1. They are afraid it won't get done.
>
> 2. They are afraid it won't get done the right way,
>   i.e., THEIR WAY!

I suspect it's more of number two. We don't delegate for fear that it won't be done OUR WAY. Funny thing is, most of the time, it doesn't need to be done OUR WAY. It just needs to be DONE! We assume a measure of personal control that is unnecessary.

Here are three excellent tips for delegating without regret.

> 1. Clearly explain the job; including all steps needed for completion, the deadline, and the desired outcome.
>
> 2. Establish open lines of communication. For example: "I expect you to ask me lots of questions—none are too big or too small or silly."
>
> 3. Set regular intervals to check on the progress. "I'll check in with you in three days (or three hours) to see how it's going."

The most important thing to remember about delegation is that you are not just "dumping" a task on someone else. You still have some interaction with it, while not carrying the majority of the burden of the work.

I know you are thinking, "Delegation is so much work. I could have just done it myself." And this may be true. However, look at the bigger picture:

1. You have now taught someone else a new skill/task and he will need less training on the next project.

2. You let your co-worker feel important by trusting her with this task.

3. You freed up some of your time allowing you to attend to other things.

4. You have started a good work habit.

People who learn to delegate do it often. It allows them to be more effective and creates a positive and trusting work environment.

✛ Praise, Encourage or Demand Accountability
I love this tip! Ever since we first blamed our dog for eating our homework, we have gotten into the habit of blaming others for our own missteps. There is always someone or something else to blame.

"This report is late because accounting didn't give me the figures." Or, "The shipment was incorrect because the computer accidentally doubled the order." Or, fill in your own excuse here: "_____."

We need to bring a sense of responsibility and accountability back to the workplace. The buck should stop with you. And probably start with you as well!

If you are in a management position, it is possible for you to create a culture of accountability with your staff. Remove the fear of retribution that may subconsciously encourage employees to blame. Help employees to feel empowered and to take action without fear of repercussion.

If you are not a manager, determine for yourself how you can be more accountable for your own actions. Choose to take ownership of both your successes and failures. This will free you from fear, and allow you to be more focused and productive.

> "The best advice you ever gave me was to take a deep breath, step back, and prioritize! It is difficult for me to deal with people who are not held accountable for their actions. So I am taking a number of deep breaths these days!"
> Bobbie Wittmer,
> Retired Director of Student
> Activities, Illinois Central College

✛ Train and Cross-Train Employees

Have you ever covered the phones for a colleague or offered to do something else on their behalf? Chances are you were cross-trained. Cross-training simply means allowing someone else the opportunity to learn some elements of your job. This has great potential to reduce chaos for you.

When there are a couple of other folks who know the essential elements of your job, it releases a great weight from you. Often without you realizing it.

Lately I've had several people tell me that they haven't gone on vacation in many years because no one knows how to do their job. Frankly, to me this seems extreme. Think of the positive benefits to having others know your job.

1. You can take vacations, feeling confident that things will be accomplished.

2. You will feel great that someone else knows what a pain your job can be (don't underestimate the value of this!)

3. The old, "If you are hit by a bus" theory, knowing that work will continue even if you aren't there.

Pick one or two key tasks and one or two trusted and logical co-workers to begin cross-training. Be clear in outlining the tasks and details to successfully accomplish the job. Praise and recognize these folks for successfully training and implementing the new skills. Keep some documentation available for core tasks in case of extended absences. And then TAKE YOUR VACATION! (Send me a postcard!)

✛ Identify Hidden Resources

My dear friend, Karen was recently given the task of inputting data from a 28-page survey into the computer in addition to the duties she already had. She was overwhelmed by the thought of the 150 surveys she had in front of her until she realized that she had some hidden resources that might be available to her.

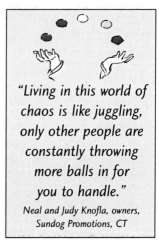

In fact, she was able to secure the assistance of one staff member who was on restricted duty due to a temporary medical condition. He turned out to be very well suited to data entry. She also found the evening receptionist had extra time and an available computer, so she enlisted her help as well.

"Living in this world of chaos is like juggling, only other people are constantly throwing more balls in for you to handle."

Neal and Judy Knofla, owners, Sundog Promotions, CT

Karen relayed this to me with a smile I had not seen since she first learned she had to coordinate this project. She found additional resources and that has made all of the difference.

What hidden resources might you have if you take the time to look for them? Perhaps your supervisor has a pool of money that you can tap into, or there is additional storage for some key equipment in a janitorial closet. Maybe you have someone who dabbles in graphic arts as a hobby and can then design your next newsletter.

There are resources around you, if you take the time to look for them. Better yet, YOU might be a resource to someone around you. Do them a favor and offer them your services!

✤ Do The Yucky Jobs First

Did you read the tip on procrastination? Lots of times we procrastinate because we don't like something on the list. Knowing that the "dreaded task" is on the list often stops us from even approaching the list.

Do the hard, yucky or disdainful task first. Get it out of the way. Make the call to the angry customer. Solve the problem and then bask in the glow of your accomplishment as you finish the other tasks.

If the call to the customer doesn't go well, shake if off and look forward to the more benign tasks on your list. Either way it is over, and you are on to the next thing. Once you relieve the pressure from the dreaded task, you free yourself to continue working. Usually in a better mood!

✤ Keep Learning!

I meet so many people at conferences where I am invited to speak. I especially love the environment of a conference. Sure, they are typically held at unique and sometimes exotic places. A change of venue is always welcomed.

But more than the locale or facilities, I love the learning

environment. I enjoy seeing people gathered in small groups in the halls, sharing information from the workshops they have attended. I love it when they learn from me—and love hearing that they learned something from others.

 You can almost see the light bulbs going off in a room when participants are engaged. You know that ideas are popping into their heads and that things will change when they get back to their workplace. You also know that they have changed a bit too. It is very cool!

We all feel a bit more professional when we learn something new about our jobs. We like being able to say, "I was reading in our professional journal about a company that...." We like to feel competent. Committing to continuous learning helps us to feel competent.

Don't have money for conferences? Join a computer list-serve with folks who have the same job. Start a book club at lunch. Read best selling business books, or just read the newspaper and discuss an article that relates to your workplace. No matter the method, keep learning, keep growing.

✛ Network With Others

At 23, when I began my professional career, the only thing I knew for sure was how much I didn't know. Yes, I was fresh out of graduate school, where they try to teach you useful things; but, honestly, my first professional job had little relationship to my formal collegiate training.

I learned much by trial and error—especially error that first year. I also learned by watching and asking questions of those around me. Both very effective learning techniques.

But if you asked me how I really became a successful practitioner, I would have to say that it was from my extensive volunteer work for my professional association and the networking opportunities it afforded me.

I would discuss organizational business with a colleague, and then we would brainstorm ways to solve a dilemma on my campus. I would visit my colleagues at their campuses and raid their bookshelves to see what I should be reading. I  did attend lots of conferences and learned new techniques from respected presenters; but I also learned as much, if not more, at the bar after hours with my friends.

We never intentionally discussed work; it was just so much a part of our lives that the conversation naturally gravitated toward it. The opinions of my work mates played an important role in helping me to formulate my own opinions and ultimately my actions.

There are many ways to network. These organizations may host networking events and are great places to start:

---

* **The local Chamber of Commerce**

* **Your professional organization**

* **Community service groups such as: Rotary or Kiwanis**

* **A volunteer organization such as the Red Cross or Cancer Society**

Make some time to attend these events. Networking will teach you more about yourself and your job. It can also be a very good place to "vent" and let off some steam with people who totally understand because they have been there too.

✢ Take Your Breaks

Why do many unions work so hard to negotiate breaks into the workday—only to have you ignore them? Why do companies who are not legally required to offer a break to their employees? It's because your breaks are an important tool in effectively managing your workday.

Everybody needs a break. Physically, your body needs a break from the constant sitting or standing; it needs to shift positions. Other organs in your body may need some relief too!

Your brain needs a change of venue. Taking your 10/15/20 minute break allows your brain a chance to refresh. Make good use of the time. If appropriate, go outside and get some fresh air. Take a quick walk. Drink something cool and refreshing. Bring yourself a fresh perspective.

Giving your brain a break will help it refocus when you return. Your brain is just amazing. With even a short break, it will come back with some new ideas, ready to tackle the rest of the day.

➜ **TAKE YOUR BREAK**

➜ **TAKE YOUR LUNCH BREAK**

➜ **TAKE A BATHROOM BREAK**

➜*Everybody needs a BREAK!*

✢ **Prioritize**

In comedy, timing is everything! We've all seen a comedian flop because his or her timing was just a bit off.

This is also true for the workplace. Timing is everything. And figuring out whose time it is or which project gets more time is one of the most difficult of all of the organizational skills. Yet, done well, it can be the backbone of your efforts to lessen your chaos.

Remember my idea about the two-minute reflection? Well, here's where you can put it to its best use. When you clearly identify the priorities of a morning, afternoon, or whole day, you give yourself direction, purpose, and goals—all the things humans need to create action.

Your to-do list can be completely overwhelming, or it can be a wonderfully simple call to action. Prioritizing helps you decide which it is. Determining the three top priorities for your morning from a to-do list of 15 items will give you focus and direction that will allow you to get some things done.

Not to say that there won't be interruptions or changes to your priorities, as others may have influence over your time. However, you now have a goal to strive for and a place to return to after the inevitable side trip. Too, your sense of accomplishment at setting and achieving your priorities may earn you a Seinfeld size standing ovation!

✛ Take Control of Your E-mail

Possibly my biggest pet peeve with the workplace today is e-mail. I could spend hours talking about how annoying it is. But really, I see just a couple of things about e-mail that we need to address because it causes so much chaos for so many.

Volume

Employees report receiving over 100 e-mails a day. Is this reasonable? Look at your e-mail and ask yourself if there is a way to reduce it. Can you get out of some chat groups or list serves that e-mail you frequently? Are there people who send you superfluous e-mail? Ask them politely to stop. Become assertive where you can, in order to reduce the sheer volume of unwanted/unnecessary e-mails.

Immediacy

Just because I can send an e-mail in a nanosecond doesn't mean I have to respond that fast. Many issues raised on e-mail need to have a bit more consideration. Take the time needed to formulate the proper response.

If you have an audible sound alerting you to a new e-mail, shut it off. Set some limits on how often you check your e-mail.

I often counsel clients to have an automatic outgoing message that states the hours they respond to e-mail. That way they can take control of their time. If you can't do that, set a timer and answer e-mails for a set amount of time. Make sure that it fits in with your priorities for that day.

Some people, although they won't admit this, use checking e-mail as a procrastination technique to avoid doing something else. It is easy to get "lost" in the virtual world as time flies away from you.

What to do with it

I spoke to a person today who said, "I'm not good about deleting my e-mail. I let things sit in my inbox in case I need them, but it takes a while to find the messages I need." We don't do this with snail mail. All of the time management experts tell us to handle paper only once. This concept, with some tweaking, can help you manage your e-mail.

After you read a message, take action immediately, move it to a folder for pending action, or delete it. Don't keep it in your inbox—it is a psychological weight on you. You won't believe how good it will feel to have a "lighter" inbox. Just like spring cleaning—but do it more often than just in the spring!

Privacy

Because I am impertinent, I ask these questions to workshop participants when we discuss e-mail:

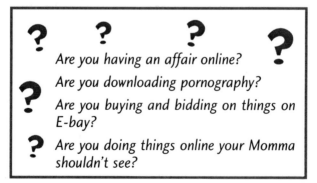

Are you having an affair online?

Are you downloading pornography?

Are you buying and bidding on things on E-bay?

Are you doing things online your Momma shouldn't see?

Invariably the answer to all of these questions is laughter and a resounding "NO!"

The follow-up question is:

So why is your e-mail so private?

You see, once the computer wizards determined we all needed a secret password for our e-mail, they created a monster that I'm sure they never envisioned.

In my early years of work, I had a wonderful administrative assistant, Pam, who sorted the snail mail. I taught her the things I liked to read, those I liked to have tossed, and how to know if something was private. It took a while but worked very well for eleven years.

When I even mention allowing someone else e-mail access, eyebrows raise, and looks of incredulity follow. I realize in some places, this is not possible. But in others it is. Give it a try!

Start small. Create a temporary password and give someone you trust access while you are on vacation. They can attend to some details while you are away, delete unnecessary messages and prioritize the e-mails that you should deal with quickly upon your return.

I can hear the objections flying around! "Here's why I can't...." I'm just asking you to realize that e-mail, like snail mail and voice mail, *is only a tool* to help you do your job. It should not be the burden it has so obviously become. Take control of your e-mail!

✦ Be Realistic About Your Operational Style

Do you have beautiful color-coded files? Is your desk as neat as a pin? Can you find virtually anything requested without breaking a sweat?

If you answered yes to any of these questions then you are the exact opposite of me—and about half of the rest of the world.

I applaud neat, organized people. One of my best friends is the most organized person I have ever met. I dream of living in a world where I always know where my keys are. But that's all it is for me, a dream. I realize this about myself. How about you?

How do you typically react when you are under pressure? Do you suddenly feel the need to become super organized? Do you fight your natural urges and try to become someone you are not?

It takes more energy, both physical and mental, to try and reinvent yourself under pressure. And when you do, it doesn't usually last. This can lead to feelings of inadequacy and low self-esteem.

There is no need for this. Be gentle with yourself. Understand that your operational style is unique to you and part of what makes you so awesome.

However, your style may contribute to your chaos. Once you acknowledge this, you can develop ways to overcome some of the ill effects.

For instance, if you are continually late and have to be on time to an event, use your natural sense of competition to make a goal of being on time. If your filing system is "management by piles," make a point to know what is in each of your piles and celebrate when you can find something quickly.

Don't try to hold yourself up to someone else's standards of neatness, organization or time management. Make the most of who you already are.

"Chaos helps you keep your character in check."
Lynne Delio, One who has been there and done that!

Try One New Thing— Do it Regularly

This book has provided you with nearly fifty tips to help you thrive during chaotic times in your life. You've read it, nodded your head and laughed, or said, "No way, no can do!" For some of you, it may seem a bit overwhelming. Don't let it be.

Every time I teach, I present lots of new material and many, many ways to incorporate it into your life. But I really want participants to adopt just *one new thing* to get them started.

Twenty years of experience as a consultant have taught me that people cannot implement fifty new ways of living and working all at once. If they try to do this, in their enthusiasm to change, usually nothing really changes.

But, if I can get them to do one thing differently—and do it regularly—I know that change will occur. Lasting and meaningful change.

Pick something in this book you want to work on: maybe your e-mail, or delegation, or asking your family to help around the house. Incorporate this one tip into your life. Try it out. Maybe it will work for you. If not, try something else. After all, life is not an exact science! But try something! Because if you feel that chaos is in control of your life, you owe it to yourself to make a change that just might be one for the better.

I want you to thrive—to continue to grow and fully enjoy your life—in all of its craziness. I don't want the chaos to rob you of the joy that is possible for you.

> *"Chaos is a reality in everyone's life...
> the secret is to THRIVE
> in that chaos - that's
> where success
> and happiness occur!"*
>
> Brian Gardner, Program Coordinator,
> Student Involvement,
> Maryville University of St. Louis

Your Thriving Action Plan

You've stuck with me so far. Good for you! Now it's time to take all that you've learned and create a plan of action for thriving in your chaos. The following questions will be important to help you understand the nature of your chaos and places you might be able to make some changes. Don't skip this work! It is an essential part of creating lasting and meaningful change in your life. In this first section, focus on your personal life. There will be another section to focus on your professional life.

Thriving in Your Personal Life

- *The Assessment* -

Let's fully assess your situation before you select a thriving method. Please answer the following questions.

What is it about your life that makes it chaotic in the first place? List five things that contribute to your chaos.

1. _____
2. _____
3. _____
4. _____
5. _____

Is there anything different this year from previous years?

_____

_____

_____

What are you doing that brings more chaos into your life? List at least three things.

1. _____
2. _____
3. _____

Which element of your chaos would you first like to focus on?

_____

Please write a paragraph describing the impact of this area on you. Pay special attention to the personal and emotional implications for you. _____

_____

_____

_____

_____

What elements of this situation do you have control over and can change? _____

_____

_____

What elements of this situation do you have NO control over and cannot change? _____

_____

_____

What resources might be available to you as you make some changes? _____

_____

_____

Who else might be involved or impacted as you make a change?

_____

_____

How will you feel if you are able to make a change in this area?

_____

_____

_____

_____

- *The Plan* -

You have now learned many new thriving tips to incorporate into your life. Changing even one of your chaos causing behaviors by using one of these tips will bring you closer to thriving. As you review your assessment, select one of the following tips to implement.

- General Thriving Tips -

❏ Ask More Questions

❏ Ask for Help

❏ Offer Help to Others

❏ Develop Systems to Help You Manage the Chaos

❏ Take Time for Reflection

❏ Set Some Limits

❏ Keep Your Eye on the Prize

❏ Seek Balance

❏ Thrive. Don't Just Cope

❏ See "Everyday" Humor

❏ Simplify, Simplify, Simplify

❏ Take Life Enhancing Risks

- Thriving Tips -

Thriving Tips for Your Personal Life

- ❏ Take Time for Yourself
- ❏ Change What's Not Working
- ❏ Develop a Hobby
- ❏ Say "No" More Often
- ❏ Laugh a Lot
- ❏ Be Honest About Your Strengths and Weaknesses
- ❏ Exercise
- ❏ Seek Support From Friends
- ❏ Own Your Attitude
- ❏ Get Some Sleep
- ❏ Absolve Yourself of Guilt
- ❏ Hire Some Services
- ❏ Be Flexible
- ❏ Take Care of Your Health
- ❏ Volunteer For Something
- ❏ Celebrate Good Times
- ❏ Stop Procrastinating
- ❏ Set Realistic Goals

Tip To Implement: _____

Explain what you hope to achieve by implementing this tip.

_____

_____

_____

Where will you find support as you implement this change?

_____

_____

List the obstacles you will have to overcome in order to fully implement this tip. _____

_____

_____

Is there a person or persons who will object to you making this change? _____

How will you handle this? _____

_____

_____

How will you know when you are successful? _____

_____

_____

Choose a date to begin implementing _____

What is your first step? _____

_____

_____

- *Implementation* -

Complete this section only *after* you have begun to implement the thriving tip.

How did you feel as you started to implement this change?

_____

_____

_____

Can you envision it making a difference? _____

_____

_____

Was this the right place to start making the change?
Why or why not?_____

_____

_____

_____

How have those around you reacted to this change?

_____

_____

How have you reacted to them?_____

_____

_____

_____

- *Evaluation* -

Complete this section after you have had some experience implementing your change.

Can you feel yourself growing because of this change?

_____

Were you able to be consistent in implementing this change? Why or why not? _____

_____

_____

_____

What's the next tip to implement? _____

_____

When will you start? _____

Who will you share your success with? _____

_____

_____

Thriving in Your Professional Life

These questions mirror the ones you answereed for your personal life. Please reflect on your job and idenitfy where the chaos is in your work life. Then, develop a plan to thrive at work.

- *The Assessment* -

Let's fully assess your situation before you select a thriving method. Please answer the following questions.

What is it about your life that makes it chaotic in the first place? List five things that contribute to your chaos.

1. _____
2. _____
3. _____
4. _____
5. _____

Is there anything different this year from previous years?

_____

_____

_____

What are you doing that brings more chaos into your life? List at least three things.

1. _____
2. _____
3. _____

Which element of your chaos would you first like to focus on?

_____

Please write a paragraph describing the impact of this area on you in the workplace. Pay special attention to the personal and emotional implications for you. _____

_____

_____

_____

_____

What elements of this situation do you have control over and can change? _____

_____

_____

What elements of this situation do you have NO control over and cannot change? _____

_____

_____

What resources might be available to you as you make some changes?

_____

_____

Who else might be involved or impacted as you make a change?

_____

_____

How will you feel if you are able to make a change in this area?

_____

_____

_____

_____

- The Plan -

You have now learned many new thriving tips to incorporate into your life. Changing even one of your chaos causing behaviors by using one of these tips will bring you closer to thriving. As you review your assessment, select one of the following tips to implement.

- General Thriving Tips -

❏ Ask More Questions

❏ Ask for Help

❏ Offer Help to Others

❏ Develop Systems to Help You Manage the Chaos

❏ Take Time for Reflection

❏ Set Some Limits

❏ Keep Your Eye on the Prize

❏ Seek Balance

❏ Thrive. Don't Just Cope

❏ See "Everyday" Humor

❏ Simplify, Simplify, Simplify

❏ Take Life Enhancing Risks

– Thriving Tips –

Thriving Tips for Your Professional Life

- ❑ Find a Mentor
- ❑ Identify Hidden Resources
- ❑ Be Proactive
- ❑ Keep Learning
- ❑ Don't Personalize Job Criticisms
- ❑ Take Your Breaks
- ❑ Find Your Internal Motivation
- ❑ Do the Yucky Jobs First
- ❑ Become Technically Proficient
- ❑ Network With Others
- ❑ Delegate
- ❑ Praise, Encourage or Demand Accountability
- ❑ Prioritize
- ❑ Train or Cross Train Employees
- ❑ Take Control of Your Email
- ❑ Be Realistic About Your Operational Style

Tip To Implement: _____

Explain what you hope to achieve by implementing this tip.

_____

_____

_____

Where will you find support as you implement this change?

_____

_____

List the obstacles you will have to overcome in order to fully implement this tip. _____

_____

_____

Is there a person or persons who will object to you making this change?

_____

How will you handle this? _____

_____

_____

What role does your supervisor play in helping you to implement this change? _____

_____

_____

How will you know when you are successful? _____

_____

_____

Choose a date to begin implementing _____

What is your first step? _____
_____
_____

- *Implementation* -

Complete this section only *after* you have begun to implement the thriving tip.

How did you feel as you started to implement this change?

_____
_____
_____

Can you envision it making a difference? _____
_____
_____

Was this the right place to start making the change?
Why or why not?_____
_____
_____

How have those around you reacted to this change? _____
_____
_____

How have you reacted to them?_____
_____

- *Evaluation* -

Complete this section after you have had some experience implementing your change.

Can you feel yourself growing because of this change?

_____

Were you able to be consistent in implementing this change?
Why or why not? _____

_____

_____

_____

What's the next tip to implement? _____

_____

When will you start? _____

Who will you share your success with? _____

_____

_____

Help Me Write the Next Book!
"More Thriving Tips!"

This book has helped you to understand the chaos in your life and has, I hope, provided you with many useful suggestions to help you thrive! Now it's time to write the sequel! Let's do it together.

Send me your tips for thriving in your chaos. Do you go to happy hour every Friday or take your sweetheart on a date every other week? Do you jog at 5 a.m., or write poetry? Let me know. I look forward to putting together a book with all of your suggestions to help others thrive.

Send your tips to me care of the Thriving in Chaos website, www.thrivinginchaos.com, or send this form to me at P.O. Box 833, St. Cloud MN 56302

Name _____

Title (as it may appear in the book) _____

How may we contact you with questions? (email, phone #, etc.)

_____

Thriving Tip_____

_____

_____

How does it make you feel when you are doing this?

_____

_____

Do you recommend this to others? Why/why not?

_____

_____

References

1. Bureau of Labor Statistics (www.bls.gov), ftp://ftp.bls.gov/pub/news.release/famee.txt

2. Self Storage Industry Fact Sheet, Self Storage Association,
   http://www.selfstorage.org/pdf/FactSheet.pdf April 19, 2007

3. Donna Smallin, .contributing editor, eons e-newlsetter
   http://www.eons.com/love/feature/yourself/qa-decluttering-your-life/3868

4. Johann Wolfgang von Goethe quotes (German Playwright, Poet, Novelist and Dramatist.
   1749-1832)

5. http://www.researchandmarkets.com/reportinfo.

6. http://www.tylenol.com/page.jhtml?id=tylenol/hdache/subftension.inc

7. http://www.amtamassage.org/pdf/2006consumer_survey_factsheet.pdf

8. http://www.aacp.net/images/FutureofChiropracticRevisited.pdf

9. International Spa Association, ISPA website www.experienceispa.com/ISPA

10. Kate Mulligan, "Employers Start to See Link Between Health, Productivity. Psychiatric
    News," May 3, 2002 Vol 37 number 9. American Psychiatric Association

11. http://www.divorcereform.org/rates.html
    National Center for Health Statistics, Monthly Vital Statistics Report. Nov. 30, 2004.

12. The Pew Internet & American Life Project.
    http://www.commondreams.org/headlines04/1012-02.htm

13. World Volunteer Web Newsletter. July 29, 2006

14. http://www.stateofthenewsmedia.org/narrative_newspapers_audience.asp

15. Sara Boatman, "Lessons From an Illness," National Association for Campus Activities
    PROfile Newsletter,December 1989, p.2.

16. Tom Peters, The Pursuit of WOW! Every Person's Guide to Topsy-Turvy Times.
    Vintage Books, NY 1994.

17. Dictionary.com

18. Hamlet, Act III, Scene III, William Shakespeare. about.com.

19. The National Sleep Foundation Fact Sheet www.sleepfoundation.org

Host a Thriving In Chaos Event for Your Organization!

Do your employees need to learn to thrive in their chaos? You can bring Tracy's inspiring and dynamic program, Thriving In Chaos, to your organization.

Utilizing a highly interactive format, this program demonstrates the challenges of balancing work with everyday life. Your participants will walk away with valuable tools to live more productive and fulfilling lives.

"Tracy Knofla's energy, enthusiasm, and positive message created a dynamic presentation which contributed to the overall success of the conference."
- Tri-County Action Program, St. Cloud, MN

Thriving In Chaos

❖ Is interactive, lively, and fun

❖ Creates many teachable moments

❖ Works perfectly for in-services, conferences, ongoing training initiatives, and keynote presentations

Tracy will work with you to plan the details of your program and customize a presentation to meet the needs of your participants. Let Tracy teach your staff to make small changes that will make a big difference, by hosting a Thriving in Chaos event today!

For more information on scheduling and planning your program, call High Impact Training at 320.259.8222 and visit the website www.ThrivingInChaos.com.

www.HighImpactTraining.net

Tracy Knofla and Mark Geller founded High Impact Training in 1995 in order to offer customized learning experiences and superior service to the higher education, corporate, and non-profit marketplaces nationwide.

Our company is committed to changing people's lives and creating a learning environment in which participants are powerfully engaged. Through compelling, on-site facilitation, our consultants promote positive and lasting change within your organization.

We work with our clients to design training programs based on the current needs of their organization. All training experiences are designed to empower and inspire participants to reach their maximum potential.

Subscribe to Tracy's free e-newsletter!

To receive Tracy's Thriving In Chaos Tips,
including more pearls of wisdom,
subscribe to her monthly e-newsletter at
www.ThrivingInChaos.com.